Legal Issues in Criminal Justice

The Courts

Edited By

SLOAN T. LETMAN, J.D.

DAN W. EDWARDS, PH.D.

DANIEL J. BELL, PH.D.

PILGRIMAGE
A Division Of Anderson Publishing Co.
Cincinnati, Ohio

CJ Criminal Justice Studies

LEGAL ISSUES IN CRIMINAL JUSTICE:
The Courts

ISBN: 0-932930-59-x

Cover design by Jonathan Donehoo

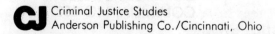
Criminal Justice Studies
Anderson Publishing Co./Cincinnati, Ohio

PREFACE

This book provides an anthology of issues from diverse perspectives. The editors conclude that a vast amount of the knowledge concerning these issues originates from a limited number of authors and publications. In this context it is important for readers to become acquainted with these issues from varied viewpoints.

The text does not include all legal issues in criminal justice. However, it incorporates selections which present the central issues in the legal and court processes. An examination of these contributions heightens the reader's insight into and appreciation for the complexities of legal issues in contemporary criminal justice.

The text is presented in eight chapters:"The First Amendment Limitations on Closure of Judicial Proceedings"focuses upon the interrelationship between defendants, the criminal justice system, and their contribution to the application of the First Amendment. The analysis is directed toward the development of judicial doctrines balancing the First Amendment right to access with the defendant's right to a fair trial and security considerations in correctional institutions. The result of a balanced approach has been to require reasonable limitations on information access. The *Richmond Newspapers* decision analyzes the opinions on the judicial right of access and discusses the ramifications of the decision in the context of future access, reasonable limitations, and what findings are sufficient to constitute overriding interests supporting information closure.

"The Supreme Court and Development of Federal Habeas Corpus Doctrine" addresses the writ of habeas corpus as loosely defined and rests primarily on its English common law origins. The greatest importance of the writ of habeas corpus is that within the federal system of government it provides a means of collateral review, i.e., pursuing judicial relief in both the state and federal court systems. The material presents a perspective of changing attitudes and policies of the United States Supreme Court in the area of review of state court decisions through application of the writ of habeas corpus. The application of habeas corpus is reviewed from the Judiciary Act of 1789 through the Post-Warren Era of the Supreme Court. The analysis of the federal habeas corpus doctrine provides valuable insight into the place of the Supreme Court in the criminal justice system, its relation to other courts, and its role in the historical evolution of habeas corpus review.

"Pre-Trial Diversion: Continuing Constitutional Concerns" emphasizes alternatives from the increased use of summons and citations in certain cases entering into mediation and/or arbitration in other cases, and increased utilization of restitution as creative resolutions in lieu of prosecution via the conventional criminal process. In analysis of the development of diversion cases, any pretrial diversion program involving court-related matters should be structured so that the individual's rights are not in jeopardy. Generally, diversion programs have operated with only limited legal challenge with regard to violations of constitutional rights. However, the growth of court cases in this area suggests a need for more detailed legislative, judicial, and administrative definitions of the rights of pretrial diversion participants.

"The Dilemma of Legal Versus Moral Responsibility and the Insanity Defense" contends that there is a difference between legal and moral responsibility and examines the ethical, moral, and practical controversies surrounding the insanity defense. The authors present arguments for both retention and abolition of the defense. Recognizing that our system of justice is founded on the notion of free will and individual responsibility a brief historical overview of the insanity defense is included. The relationship of free will, determinism, and individual culpability are examined in the context of four legal tests of insanity. The analysis focuses attention on criminal intent or the lack thereof as a mitigating factor in the establishment of moral responsibility. The tenuous association between psychiatry and the law as they relate to the insanity defense is examined, the moral and ethical dilemmas that the present state of scientific knowledge present to our system of justice when dealing with mentally disordered defendants are delineated, and the question of whether a society has the moral right to punish its mentally disordered offenders is addressed, with special attention given to the notion of guilty but insane.

"Plea Bargaining: Contradiction or Justice?" proposes that when "justice" is evaluated by each offender answering for their actions it is difficult to determine how plea bargaining serves justice. The inconsistencies in plea bargaining have caused a loss of public confidence in government, increased the possibility of corruption in the prosecutor's office, negated the intent of the legislatures, and permitted poor bargains to be made by inexperienced or careless prosecutors. Thus neither the defendants who received a reduced sentence for a less serious offense than they actually committed or the innocent individuals who were negotiated into guilty pleas have received justice. More importantly, however, society has not received justice. Society has a right to expect convicted offenders to be punished to the extent the law allows and innocent individuals to be treated as such. The plea bargaining process has negated these expectations.

"Capital Punishment: Recurring Issues" presents a review of capital punishment issues: constitutionality, morality, justice, and the effectiveness of capital punishment. A consistent consideration in the capital punishment controversy has been the perception of the threat of punishment. In reality, the rate of criminal occurrances has increased while the corresponding rate of punishment has decreased. In the past, this has been considered evidence of an increased opportunity to commit criminal acts or evidence of a society where the criminal justice system has displayed more interest in protecting law violators than it has in protecting victims. Although capital punishment has been discussed for decades, it remains one of the most controversial issues in contemporary society.

"Law and Ethics" discusses the professional role of the lawyer and the responsibilities implicit in such a role, posits the issue of how the lawyer is to resolve conflicts which may develop between his role as an officer of the court and his moral responsibility as a citizen. The purpose of this chapter is to show that when a lawyer is acting as an officer of the court, the dilemma must necessarily be solved on the side of the law, even if the law conflicts with his sense of responsibilities as a human being and concerned citizen. The chapter is organized according to attorneys and the various roles they played in regard to ex-president Richard M. Nixon and Watergate. The material is presented through a discussion of Nixon followed by the major Watergate participants. There is an additional dilemma in the legal profession. Laws are inflexible and cannot be changed, except by men, and when they do change, the change always lags behind the moral sensibilities of men.

"Contemporary Issues and Trends in Court Reform" presents a discussion of the reform efforts that have attempted to increase the efficiency and effectiveness of our federal and state court systems. Among the more prominent efforts supported by reformers are court unification, merit selection of the judiciary, and increased use of technology in the courts. Court unification offers a means to eliminate waste and enhance coordination in state judicial systems. Merit selection of the judiciary offers a means to select more highly qualified judges apart from the contemporary political practices. Although great hope for reform is placed in each of these efforts, little empirical research has been conducted to establish the validity of the claims of their proponents. On the other hand, videotaping offers promise for improved court proceedings in keeping with the advances of modern technology.

The selections are equally valuable to professionals, researchers, and students seeking additional knowledge and understanding regarding the development and application of legal issues in the criminal justice system. The value of the text to criminal justice educators and professionals is in its candid discussion of issues in the field. The legal issue topics, although condensed, are a desirable basis for the understanding needed by criminal justice practioners.

CONTENTS

FIRST AMENDMENT LIMITATIONS ON CLOSURE OF JUDICIAL PROCEEDINGS

> Congress shall make no law respecting an establishment of religion, or prohibiting the free exercise thereof; or abridging the freedom of speech, or of the press; or the right of people peaceably to assemble, and to petition the Government for a redress of grievances.
> - U.S. Constitution, Amendment 1.

There is no explicit language granting public and press access to judicial proceedings in this First Amendment of the United States Constitution. As a result, the path leading to judicial recognition of a public and press First Amendment right to attend criminal trials has been a long and arduous one. Upon looking at the development of judicial doctrine in the First Amendment area, it is apparent that this treatment of compromise and balancing of a First Amendment right has consistently appeared when the issue posed is "access" to information, more often than when the issue posed is content and dissemination of the same information. This pattern seems to be centered around the interpretation of the First Amendment press clause and the historic characterization of the "openness" of the place for which public access is sought.

Does the First Amendment merely give the press as an institution the right to publish and disseminate information without infringement from law or judicial order, or does the Amend-

ment go even further and give the press the
additional right to acquire newsworthy information based on the public's right to know without
infringement? Where the issue posed has been
the press' right to publish and disseminate information concerning a judicial proceeding or be
subject to prior restraint, gag orders or contempt proceedings in the interest of a fair administration of justice, the U.S. Supreme Court
has consistently upheld the press' right to publish. The Court has adhered to this categorical
rule even when the press commented upon and
criticized pending litigation[1] or the press
criticized and abused judges engaged in the decision of lawsuits,[2] or the press printed
criticism of a grand jury by an elected sher-
iff[3] or the press divulged the name of a judge
whose fitness was being investigated by a judicial commission in violation of a state confidentiality statute.[4]

However, when the issue posed has been the
right of the press to "acquire" newsworthy information, rather than promulgating a categorical rule, the Court has used a balancing approach that thereby subjects this aspect of the
First Amendment right to state and judicial regulation and possible curtailment. Even when the
information is being sought from a place characterized as historically "open" whether regulation or prohibition can be justified will be determined by a balancing approach as in the
speech and assembly cases. While access to historically "open" places such as streets,
parks,[5] and state capital grounds[6] for the
enjoyment of First Amendment rights could be
regulated, but not prohibited using a balanced
approach, access to places not historically

"open" such as jails could be prohibited by a categorical rule.[7] This position has subsequently been reversed in *Gayned v. Rockford*[8] so that the reasonableness of a regulation will be determined by the pattern of normal activities of the place and must be narrowly tailored rather than determined exclusively by the historical characterization of the place.[9]

It is this balancing approach that the Court adheres to in *Richmond Newspapers, Inc. v. Commonwealth*[10] whereupon it recognizes the First Amendment right of access to criminal trials, not as an absolute right, but a right that can be limited or curtailed with proper circumstances shown. This decision, as well as the more recent *Chandler v. Florida*[11] is particularly significant to the criminal defendant on trial. A defendant's mere request to exclude public or press or an objection to an open trial will no longer be deemed sufficient to close a trial. The perennial blanket cry of "denial of due process" will not be sufficient, since the Court makes clear in both decisions that the public and press presence at total does not constitute denial of due process *pro se*, more has to be shown. These decisions reflect the growing attitude of this Supreme Court and the attitude of the country that defendants have enough rights to protect them.

This chapter will focus on how this attitude about defendants in the criminal justice system has contributed to the development of First Amendment theory. Part I addresses the development of judicial doctrine balancing First Amendment right to access with other competing interests, such as the defendant's right to a fair trial or the security interests in prisons. The result of this balancing approach has at best been to require reasonable and not arbitrary limitations and at worst, to deny access altogether. Part II reviews the decision of *Richmond Newspapers* and analyzes the opinions on the judicial right of access, while Part III, the conclusion, will discuss the ramifications of the decision in light of access cases to come.

Part I - Judicial Doctrine Limiting Access to Information Due to Competing Interests

A. *Criminal Trials*

The respect of the Supreme Court for the practice of conducting criminal prosecutions in open court is not to be doubted. As stated in *In re Oliver*[12] "(t)he Sixth Amendment reflects the traditional Anglo-American distrust for secret trials[13] and to conduct entire criminal trials in secret is a menace to liberty."[14] Further the Court held that the Sixth Amendment is an expression of our belief that the "knowledge that every criminal trial is subject to contemporaneous review in the forum of public opinion is an effective restraint on possible abuse of judicial power."[15] This constitutional right to a public trial is not, however, a limitless imperative.[16]

> Just as a government may impose reasonable time, place and manner restrictions upon the use of its streets in the interest of such objectives as the free flow of traffic, see, e.g., *Cox v. New*

Hampshire, 312 U.S. 569 (1941), so may a trial judge, in the interest of the fair administration of justice, impose reasonable limitations on access to a trial.[17]

Such limitations have been categorized into two types of competing interests by one commentator: "those based on the need to maintain order and dignity in the courtroom, and those grounded in concerns about the content of information made public."[18] The limitations that can be imposed to satisfy the court's interest in maintaining order and dignity, or the preservation of decorum may affect not only the admission of the public and press to the courtroom, but restrictions may in addition be placed upon the behavior of the audience once admitted. Thus a judge may desire to limit the number of people allowed into the courtroom to the available seating, leaving space available for those with special concerns, such as closely associated with the parties[19] may desire to restrict talking among the members of the audience to ensure the testimony is easily heard; may desire to remove not only disruptive spectators, but disruptive defendants[20] may bar the use of cameras or flashbulbs to avoid distracting the jury and witnesses[21] and so forth.[22]

1. *Limitations to Maintain Courtroom Decorum*

The need for many or most of these limitations can be found illustrated by the "carnival atmosphere" of the trial of *Sheppard v. Maxwell*.[23] Justice Clark wrote of the spectacle:

The fact is that bedlam reigned at the courthouse during the trial and newsmen took over practically the entire court-room, hounding most of the participants in the trial, especially Sheppard. At a temporary table within a few feet of the jury box and counsel table sat some 20 reporters staring at Sheppard and taking notes. The erection of a press table for reporters inside the bar is unprecedented .... Having assigned almost all of the available seats in the courtroom to the news media the judge lost his ability to supervise that environment. The movement of the reporters in and out of the court-room caused frequent confusion and dis-ruption of the trial. And the record re-veals constant commotion within the bar. Moreover, the judge gave the throng of newsmen gathered in the corridors of the courthouse absolutely free rein. Partic-ipants in the trial, including the jury, were forced to run a gauntlet of report-ers and photographers each time they en-tered or left the courtroom. The total lack of consideration for the privacy of the jury was demonstrated by the assign-ment to a broadcasting station of space next to the jury room on the floor above the courtroom, as well as the fact that jurors were allowed to make telephone calls during their five-day deliberation.

Noting that the trial court's fundamental error was the holding that it "lacked power to control the publicity about the trial,"[24] and that the judge "never considered other means that are often utilized to reduce the appearance of prejudicial material and to protect the jury from outside influence,"[25] Justice Clark insisted that "the cure lies in those remedial measures that will prevent the prejudice at its inception, and that (t)he courts must take such steps by rule and regulation that will protect their processes from prejudicial outside interferences."[26]

He went further and suggested some proper rules and regulations[27] that trial judges should follow:

> 1. Limit the number of reporters in the courtroom itself at the first sign that their presence would disrupt the trial and regulate their conduct while in the courtroom, i.e., admonish them not to handle and photograph trial exhibits lying on counsel table during recesses.
>
> 2. Insulate the witnesses from press interviews.
>
> 3. Impose control over the statements made to the news media by counsel, witnesses, and especially the coroner and police officers.
>
> 4. Proscribe extrajudicial statements by any lawyer, party, witness, or court official which divulged prejudicial matters, such as refusal to submit to interrogation or take any lie detector tests; any statements made to officials; the identity of prospective witnesses or their probable testimony; any belief in guilt or innocence; or like statements concerning the merits of the case.
>
> 5. Where there is a reasonable likelihood that prejudicial news prior to a

trial will prevent a fair trial, the judge should continue the case until the threat abates, or transfer it to another county not so permeated with publicity.

6. Sequestration of the jury.

7. If publicity during the proceedings threatens the fairness of the trial, a new trial should be ordered.

Concluding that these procedures would have been sufficient to guarantee a fair trial, Justice Clark expressly chose not to "consider what sanctions might be available against a racalcitrant press...."[28]

The need to bar or limit the use of cameras, particularly television cameras, can be illustrated by the problem posed in *Estes v. Texas*.[29] The problem for the Supreme Court, in deciding to reverse Estes' conviction, involved both the physical disruption caused by the camers, lights and wires, and the emotional impact of television's presence by its very nature. In Justice Clark's opinion for the Court, he wrote:

> The freedom granted to the press under the First Amendment must be subject to the maintenance of absolute fairness to the judicial process; and in the present state of television technology, such freedom does not confer the right to use equipment in the courtroom which might jeopardize a fair trial, the atmosphere for which must be preserved at all costs.[30]

At the time of *Estes*, only two states, Texas and Colorado, allowed television in the courtroom. The problems in *Estes* did not do much to encourage more states to allow television cameras in courts. Today, twenty-five states, including Ohio, are experimenting or have experimented with cameras in the court.[31] Courts once participating in the experiment set up guidelines and conditions and limitations for television camera access to trials. The Florida plan is probably representative of workable and realistic guidelines set up to handle the practical problem of courtroom filming:

> No permission was required of any party to a court action. All equipment (for radio and television) was pooled, only noiseless cameras were allowed, and all equipment had to remain stationary in the back of the room. Only existing lighting was used.[32]

These two cases, *Estes v. Texas* and *Sheppard v. Maxwell*, posed the challenge of free press/fair trial in such a fashion that in addition to the fact that the gains of the contempt cases could have been lost, access to judicial proceedings could also have been lost on due process grounds. Given that Justice Frankfurter had advocated only a few years before in his concurrence in *Irwin v. David* that controlling the press rather than reversal of convictions would be an appropriate remedy for prejudicial publicity, leaving no doubt of his readiness to permit the states to employ the contempt power against publications that interferred with pending judicial proceedings, the majorities in *Estes* and *Sheppard* must be commended for resisting such a remedy. The television presence in *Sheppard* was so disruptive of the judicial process itself and the prejudicial publicity so damaging to the defendants (at least to Sheppard) that the Court in both cases went beyond the reversal of convictions, toward categorical rules designed to prevent prejudice by limiting certain activities of the press.[33]

These rules the Court has consistently adhered to, to insure public and press access to *trials*, particularly where trial by jury.

> Though it is clear that the court has a legitimate interest in promulgating rules of decorum, it is equally clear that any such rules may place incidental burdens on the public's right of access - burdens that cannot be ignored if the right is to have any meaning.[34]

The Court in *Richmond* addressed the issue of the "reasonableness" of the limitations on access to trial in the following terms:

> (T)he question in a particular case is whether that control is exerted so as not to deny or unwarrantedly abridge .... the opportunities for the communication of thought and the discussion of public questions immemorially associated with resort to public places.[35]

In light of the background of *Estes* and *Sheppard*, it would be very difficult to argue that the acceptable limitations promulgated by the Court in *Sheppard* and those being promulgated by courts experimenting with admission of television cameras are so burdensome that they "deny or unwarrantedly abridge .... the opportunities for the communication of thought and the discussion of public questions...."

2. Content-based restrictions

Content-based restrictions reflect the desire of the Court to restrict public access because of a concern that the information revealed by holding the trial in the open will impair one of three competing interests: the right to a fair trial, the interest in privacy, and the interest in preserving state secrets.[36] Justice Powell, in his concurring opinion in *Gannett v. DePasquale*,[37] commented:

> (The right of access to courtroom proceedings) is limited only by the constitutional right of defendants to a fair trial, and by the needs of government to obtain just convictions and to preserve the confidentiality of sensitive information and the identity of informants. The task of determining the application of these limitations in each individual trial necessarily falls almost exclusively upon the trial court asked to exclude members of the press and public from the courtroom.[38]

a. To insure the right to a fair trial

The court in *Gannett* held that the source of the defendant's right to a fair trial is the Sixth Amendment. The guarantees that this Amendment provides to a person charged with the commission of a criminal offense is *personal* to the defendant and members of the public have no enforceable Sixth Amendment right to a public trial that can be asserted independently of the parties in the litigation.

A defendant cannot be convicted if he has not been provided a fair trial, which is certainly the case if the jury is biased because of publicity. Therefore there may be a legitimate fear by the court that if the trial is held in public, the resulting publicity will influence jury members and impair the possibility of a truly fair trial. The real problem, however, is to prove that publicity does in fact affect the jury's verdict. Even in a case like *Estes*, where the trial had been televised, though the Court reversed his conviction, it was not because prejudice had been shown. As a matter of fact, the jury had not even been polled to determine how many had seen the television broadcasts. The Court in *Nebraska Press Association v. Stuart*, [39] relying upon *Stroble v. California*, [40] *Beck v. Washington*, [41] and *Murphy v. Florida* [42] noted that " *all* pervasive and adverse publicity does not inevitably lead to an unfair trial."[43] (Emphasis added.) Empirical research by lawyers and social scientists does not shed a convincing light that will sufficiently refute the *Nebraska* comment. Schmidt discusses the problem as follows:

> (N)obody knows with any precision what happens to jurors in criminal trials. Our legal system, mindful of the value of mystery to the jury's function, had not been congenial to direct observation of juries at work. Nor is it likely that the legal system would condone experimental trials in which variables could be explored through the reactions of unsuspecting juries ....

Thus, estimates of the ultimate effect of prejudicial information on jury decisions can rest only on intuition, on suppositions drawn from general knowledge about opinion formation and retention or on simulations of the jury process that attempt to test experimentally what happens to prejudice in the course of a criminal trial.[44]

Despite these shortcomings, there is little disagreement among researchers,[45] lawyers and social scientists alike, with the assumption that certain kinds of publicity create prejudice and that the report of a confession has the greatest impact, followed by information that a defendant has a prior criminal record. The Reardon Report[46] pointed to other kinds of prejudicial publicity, such as reports that an accused engaged in plea bargaining, that he refused to submit to a polygraph test, or that ballistics, fingerprints or other technical tests implicated him.[47] Such evidence, particulary confessions, ballistics reports and fingerprint evidence, is crucial to the question of guilt and will therefore likely be introduced before the actual day of trial in pre-trial hearings such as the preliminary hearing and motion to supress hearing.

(1) Pre-trial publicity
Given the empirical research to substantiate the kinds of information about a criminal case that create prejudice and the significance of that evidentiary information to the developing states of the criminal trial process, it becomes quite clear that the pre-trial states of the

criminal trial pose a particularly acute constitutional problem. Since during the pre-trial hearing stage, the jury has not been selected and the information likely to be revealed has the greatest prejudicial impact, should the public and the press have access to these hearings and thus access to prejudicial information? If the hearings are closed to the public and press, has the defendant been denied his right to a public trial and has the public and press been denied First Amendment rights? The substantive and procedural aspects of this problem had been addressed in two recent U.S. Supreme Court cases, *Gannett v. DePasquale* and *Nebraska Press Association, Inc., v. Stuart*. Ancillary problems such as access to trial documents not admitted into evidence, access to jury lists and defendant's grand jury testimony have been addressed in various state and federal cases.

In *Nebraska Press*, a suspect confessed that he murdered five of his neighbors because he was caught in a sexual act with yet another neighbor. The confession was read in open court in a *preliminary hearing* that was also open to the public and press. Because of the publicity generated due to the incident in this small Nebraska town of 750 people, local and outside media was present. The trial court thereupon enjoined publication of the confession in order to protect the defendant's right to a fair trial, and this injunction was upheld by the Nebraska courts. The U.S. Supreme Court viewed the injunction as a prior restraint and unanimously reversed the trial court's decision. Upon stating that "(p)rior restraints on speech and publication are the most serious and the least tolerable infringement on First Amendment rights,"[48] Chief Justice Burger writing for the majority declared a strict three-part test that states had to satisfy where circumstances warranted a prior restraint. Under the majority's test:

> to determine whether .... the gravity of the "evil" was discounted by its improbability justifies such invasion of free speech as is necessary to avoid the danger .... we must examine the evidence before the trial judge when the order was entered to determine:
>
> a. the nature and extent of pretrial news coverage (is it likely to be so pervasive that it will probably have an effect on jurors);
> b. whether other measures would be likely to mitigate the effects of unrestrained pretrial publicity; and
> c. how effectively a restraining order would operate to prevent the threatened danger.[49]

"In meeting the first part of the test, ... a court may not simply speculate on the effect publicity will have on jurors; it must have proof. The *Nebraska Press* trial judge was chastised for his failings on this point,"[50] having his conclusion on the prejudicial effect on prospective jurors "of necessity speculative, dealing as he was with factors unknown and unknowable."[51] In light of the empirical research confirming that the report of a confession has the greatest prejudicial impact upon the public, courts and attorneys may have to resort to taking testimony from Justice Reardon and the host of social scientists who have conducted such studies and those who are continuing to do so, to satisfy the "proof" requirement of the first part of the test.

As for consideration of alternative measures (the requirement of the second prong of the test) the most successful of the *Sheppard* alternatives of change of venue, continuance, sequestration of the jury and extensive voir dire would likely have been a combination of continuance and change of venue. At the time of the preliminary hearing, publicity had been so extensive, even in surrounding counties, that a change of venue would not have insured moving the trial to a community unfamiliar with the facts of the case. Therefore, even with a change of venue, to do so after continuing the case until such time as the publicity could have subsided, would be more effective in mitigating the effects of the publicity than the alternatives of extensive voir dire or sequestration.

The problem of voir dire is also related to the problem in the third prong of the test. In this small Nebraska town of 750 people, a restraining order would not operate to prevent the threatened danger of an unfair trial for the defendant. It would be very difficult to believe that everyone in the town did not know about the murders. Extensive voir dire could only screen those with the strongest preconceived notions of guilt or innocence, but the likelihood of getting twelve qualified jurors out of that venire is extremely slim.

The net effect of this three-part balancing test is as one commentator would describe it as being "so strict it can never be met."[52]

- 16 -

The unlikelihood of meeting this strict three-part test makes what appears to be a balanced test, in actuality, a categorical rule, which is the position that Justices Brennan, Stewart, Marshall and Stevens advocate to begin with: the proposition that there should be an absolute ban against prior restraints in the fair trial context.

Despite the fact that the majority opinion recognizes that "(n)one of our decided cases on prior restraint involved restrictive orders entered to protect a defendant's right to a fair and impartial jury ...,"[53] Justice Brennan, in his concurring opinion, began his analysis with the original prior restraint case of *Near v. Minnesota*[54] and profoundly concluded, that of the three possible exceptional circumstances whereby a prior restraint could be tolerated, prejudicial publicity to insure a fair trial was not one. Further, he could find no acceptable reason why a new fourth exception making prejudicial publicity should be created and added to the three delineated in *Near*.

What the majority opinion by posing its balancing test, while doubtful that *any* publicity would affect the selection of a jury, and the concurring opinion by advocating an absolute ban against prior restraint in the fair trial context, both fail to do, is to pointedly identify the trial judge's true sin: he attempted to abridge the press' right to publish and disseminate information. The "reason" the Court was committing the cardinal sin, the fair administration of justice, was no more relevant in this case than it was in the contempt cases. The U.S. Supreme Court has been most consistent in protecting the press as an institution from re-

strictions of law or courts that would abridge
or deny the content and dissemination of information. It has consistently adhered to the
principle that the press is free to publish
whatever information it has access to, regardless of the "source" of that information, and
has thereby allowed the publication of such controversial information as the Pentagon Papers by
the New York Times[55] and the publication of
the name of a judge whose name was protected by
a confidentiality statute that made investiga-
tions by a judicial commission private,[56] despite the fact that both sources of information
was an illegal "leak" from within the agencies
affected. Therefore, there was little need for
either opinion to have to take such pains to
conclude what judicial doctrine in the content
and dissemination has long resolved.

It is important to note that there would not
have been a prior restraint problem had the preliminary hearing not been open to the public in
the first place, unless state law so required.[57] The Supreme Court alluded to as much
while discussing the alternative measures available to the trial court. Chief Burger stated:[58]

> The County Court could not know that clo-
> sure of the preliminary hearing was an
> alternative open to it until the Nebraska
> Supreme Court so construed state law; but
> once a public hearing had been held, what
> transpired there could not be subject to
> prior restraint.

Therefore, assuming the Nebraska Supreme
Court construed Nebraska law to allow closure of
preliminary hearings, and assuming the defendant

agreed, closure of the proceeding would have survived the holding of *Nebraska Press* as an alternative to prior restraint, a tactic that gave rise to *Gannett v. DePasquale*.

Though *Gannett* addressed the issue of the pretrial suppression hearing, where no state statute authorized closure and though confusion reigned for courts throughout the country as to the meaning of the decision, one issue survived, particularly in New York and Wyoming (to name two) - the requirement of a closure hearing to balance the competing constitutional interests before determining closure.

Two recent state cases since *Gannett* involve not specifically the closing of a pretrial suppression hearing, but rather the preliminary hearing. In *Gannett Co. Inc., v. Weidman*,[59] pursuant to defense motion to close the preliminary hearing to witnesses, the media and other members of the public, and the New York Criminal Procedure Law giving the judge the discretion to close such hearings, Judge Weidman closed the hearing and in *Gannett*, the newspaper challenged the closure order claiming a First Amendment right of access. Given this decision was decided prior to the July decision of *Richmond Newspapers*, the New York Supreme Court held that First Amendment "protection does not extend to compelling the courts to fling wide their doors in *all* cases and at *all* times."[60] Further that there was under *Gannett* no Sixth Amendment right of access and as of this decision for First Amendment right to judicial or governmental proceedings. The Court went on to say, as did Justice Blackmun in *Gannett*, that "to satisfy the public interest, redacted transcripts could be made available while the defendant was still in jeopardy and pointed out that complete, unredacted transcripts (could be) made available by the trial court (once) defendant no longer in jeopardy."[61]

Despite the fact, however, there was no right of access pursuant to *Gannett* which involved a pretrial suppression hearing that was not statutorily authorized, this Court held that closure of preliminary hearing though statutorily authorized without a special hearing requirement would also be bound by the hearing requirement of *Gannett* and the procedural guidelines of *Leggett*,[62] the New York Court of Appeals case that clarified the *DePasquale* decision. The Court justifies its holding based upon the similarity between the evidence to be presented in both hearings: potentially prejudicial evidence of guilt. The Court observes:

> Preliminary hearings, like suppression hearings often involve confessions, eyewitness identifications, contraband and fruits of evidence of crimes, "the type of proof which may often be considered extremely persuasive, if not conclusive evidence of guilt."[63] The information elicited at a preliminary hearing is potentially more damaging than that brought out at a suppression hearing, inasmuch as the focus of a preliminary hearing is on the acts of the defendant, while a suppression hearing is primarily concerned with the conduct of the police in gathering evidence. Finally, the disclosures made at a preliminary hearing are not subject to verbal comment by counsel or a

ruling by the court as to their ultimate admissibility at trial and their effect as evidence of the crime charged, while suppression hearings are concerned with exactly these matters.[64]

By requiring a closure hearing before closure of a matter the law gives the trial judge the discretion to close, it is a smart move on the part of the Appellate Court. It is a recognition of the importance of the public access to *all* hearings argument that may or may not be put to rest by *Gannett* as to pretrial. These hearings to air constitutional access questions, whether the burden has been on the defendant or on the press, have been a consistent requirements from *Nebraska Press* forward, and the requirement for a record will even surface in *Richmond Newspapers*. So it seems a good idea that whenever closure is an issue, courts should be in the habit of having a thoroughly documented transcript of the pre-closure proceedings for potential review.

This is the posture taken by the Wyoming Supreme Court in *Williams v. Stafford*[65] where the provision for a pre-closure determination hearing was added to the American Bar Association Standards Relating to the Administration of Criminal Justice, Standard 8-3.2 on Fair Trial and Free Press that the court adopted to set the standards for which justice of the peace or court commissioners are required to conform in closure cases - whether preliminary hearings, bail hearings, or any other pretrial proceeding, including a motion to suppress. The ABA Standards and the Wyoming amendments require the satisfaction of the "clear and present danger to

the fairness of the trial" test. The Court got
an opportunity to review the application of its
standards by a court commissioner in *State ex
rel Feeney v. District Court of 7th Judicial District.*[66] In that case, the District Court
Judge found the court commissioner had abused
his discretion by closing the preliminary hearing after taking written motions, oral arguments
of counsel and inquiry from the Bench to form
the record supporting the commissioner's closure
decision. The Commissioner's decision to close
the preliminary hearing was based upon evidence
"inculpatory and possibly exculpatory" made by
and of the defendants, statements the County
Court did not have the jurisdiction to exclude
as inadmissible because of the Rules of Evidence, but "may well be inadmissible at a trial
on the main issue." The Supreme Court was faced
with what it will be faced with time and time
again, just as noted by the author for Justices
Blackmun's and Stewart's tests, a dispute as to
the sufficiency of the facts and whether the
Commissioner abused his discretion by closing
the hearing based upon insufficient facts. The
Wyoming Supreme Court upheld the commissioner's
closure order, which seems to indicate that if
reasonable men can differ on the same facts, the
original decision stands because the rules of
the game were followed,[67] what is left is judicial discretion. Whether a judge's discretion
will be deemed abused or not will depend upon
the whim of the observer appellate judge. Such
is not an impressive way of determining and set-
tling this access/fair trial dilemma.

Other access issues, other than access to
observe the pretrial proceeding itself, involve
access to information from trial participants
and access to sealed transcripts. In *Central*

South Carolina Chapter, Society of Professional Journalists v. *Martin* [68] newsmen, journalists, news media establishments, and a newspaper subscriber sought injunctive and declaratory relief concerning a pretrial order in a criminal case in which the trial court enjoined extrajudicial statements by "lawyers, parties, witnesses, jurors and court officials, which might divulge prejudicial matter not of public record in the case." Despite the fact that the court conceded the order restrained the trial participants from certain conduct thereby proscribing the flow of prejudicial information to be gained by nontrial participants, the court nevertheless ruled that the clear and present danger test did not apply since the order did not constitute a prior restraint on the press' or public's right to speak or publish.

Given there was access to the open hearings, given the recognition of the U.S. Supreme Court of protection of the press as an institution to publication and dissemination without government regulation, and the lack of complete support for the press' right of newsgathering[69] and finally, given the objection to the pretrial order's being a First Amendment violation came from the press and not from the trial participants themselves, these factors perhaps explain in this case by this court used the "reasonably likely" test of interference with a fair trial, a lesser standard than "clear and present danger" of interference with a fair trial. Yet the same test is used when the trial participants themselves object to such gag orders on First Amendment grounds, [70] a test only once United States Circuit Court has criticized as constituting an unconstitutional restriction on attorneys' right of free speech because it is overbroad. [71]

Where press access to sealed transcripts was sought, the decision to grant access turned on whether the pretrial proceeding had been open or closed. In *New York News, Inc., v. Bell*, [72] petitioner instituted suit to prohibit trial court from excluding the press and the public from a motion to suppress proceeding of a 13-year old defendant. The Court denied the application but in accord with the procedural requirements of the New York Court of Appeals Court in *Gannett v. DePasquale* and affirmed by the U.S. Supreme Court, the court afforded the media access to transcripts redacted to exclude matters ruled inadmissible during the closed suppression hearing. Upon objecting to the redacted transcripts, petitioner was told that the public's right to know is compatible with the defendant's right to a fair trial by access to redacted transcripts during pretrial motions and complete transcripts may be available when the defendant's interests are no longer in jeopardy.

The only consistency of law to be found on the access to sealed transcripts issue from these two cases is in both, complete transcripts are not denied indefinitely, but available once defendant's trials are concluded. Critics contend that transcripts at this point "present not news, but history."[73]

Therefore restrictions upon access will be tolerated - whether to observe the pretrial proceeding, to obtain information not of record from trial participants, or from sealed transcripts to insure a fair trial, only a prior restraint infringing a press dissemination and publication of information will not. Clearly then, this section reflects the acceptance of the court of the protection of the press as an institution, rather than the acceptance of the press' having a societal function, which entails the right of newsgathering in addition to dissemination.

(2) *At Trial*
Publicity during the actual trial once the jury is empannelled poses much less of a problem than pretrial, so long as the trial court exercises its traditional powers such as sequestration, voir dire, change of venue and continuances so as to secure a fair trial. Further, if publicity during the proceeding threatens the fairness of the trial, a new trial should be ordered.[74]

Though content-based restrictions at trial may not necessarily be solely due to publicity, there are other content-based restrictions that pose the tension between the First and Sixth Amendments, particularly when the First Amendment argument is the right of access for newsgathering. In *Nixon v. Warner Communications, Inc.*[75] broadcasters attempted to obtain "permission to copy, broadcast, and sell" to the public portions of the Nixon tapes played at the Halderman trial. The Court rejected the media's request, even though the media relied upon the *Cox Broadcasting Corp. v. Cohn*[76] holding that information made available to the public via a trial could not be kept from further distribution through the media holding that the press was not asking for access to information, but for access to the actual tapes "to which the public has never had physical access" for broadcasting, reproduction and sale. Further the court relied on a principle that will be the basis of the prison access cases as well, that "the First Amendment generally grants the press no right to information about a trial superior to that of the general public."[77]

Despite the court use of its "no special access" argument to be consistent with its own doctrine of allowing publication and dissemination of information the media can obtain from public trials, it seems the problem is the media's intent to reproduce and sell the tapes. It seems somewhat contradictory to say you can not reproduce and sell tapes, though the press can reproduce court records and sell the information in its newspapers and magazines. Perhaps the real reason the Court refused media's request was the Presidential Recordings Act which empowered the Administration of General Services to supervise the processing and release of material from the Nixon White House years. The Court noted: "The presence of an alternative means of public access tips the scales in favor of denying release, (and) the Court should not circumvent the purposes of the Act by ordering release of the tapes."[78]

The media was even more ambitious in its trial requests of evidence in *United States v. Gurney.[79]* In that case involving the trial of U.S. Senator Edward Gurney, the Fifth Circuit U.S. Court of Appeals upheld the rulings of a trial judge's denial of news media access to exhibits not yet admitted into evidence, transcripts of bench conferences held on camera, written communications between the jury and the judge, a list of names and addresses of jurors, and the defendant's grand jury testimony. The Court reasoned that "(t)he First Amendment right to gather news has been defined in terms of information available to the public generally (and t)he press cannot be denied access to any information already within the public domain."[80] Therefore the court easily concluded that because the documents sought by appellants were not part of the public record, there was no right of access.[81]

It is interesting to note in this case, though the court defines a right to gather news, it is not embracing the societal function interpretation of the press clause of that right, whereby the press "performs all the myriad tasks necessary for it to gather and disseminate the news,"[82] to provide informed public discussion. Rather, it is relying on the "no-special access" argument.

These two cases make clear there is no greater press access rights during trial than before, though the threat of harm to the fair administration of justice is lessened. No standard is needed because there is no balancing of First and Sixth Amendment rights, rather the Court finds no First Amendment rights exist.

a. *interest in privacy*

There are some instances when the witness seeks to testify in private, to protect personal dignity,[83] for fear of reprisal,[84] to testify about "highly revolting sexual practices,"[85] or if the witness is a young complainant.[86] However the dilemma posed by such instances is much greater than providing for the sensitivities of the timid or reluctant witness.

The dilemma posed requires balancing the need for full and accurate testimony with the public's interest and the defendant's interest.

There is a public interest in obtaining convictions for crimes against the state, so as to preserve order; and there is a public interest in having access to that trial to observe the administration of justice in obtaining that conviction. There is a defendant's interest in a public trial to protect himself from a proceeding in secret and to insure truth and veracity in testimony. Both the public and the defendant has an interest in a fair trial. The witness who wishes to testify in private may wish to because of the intricate details involved. On the other hand, the witness may be reluctant to testify in public because the testimony is untrue or half-true.

The court must therefore assess the value of the witness' testimony with the sacrifices to be made by the public and the defendant by yielding some of their interest. As a basic rule, where accuracy of testimony is the issue, the public and the defendant seem best served by having the the proceeding open; however even if the exceptional and overwhelming evidence is demonstrated in support of testimony in private, such a restriction should be narrowly drawn. Even before such a narrowly drawn exception, court must impress upon witnesses their tremendous responsibility to testify - they have been subpoenaed and have been placed under oath, and whether the public is present or not, they can be placed in contempt of court for refusing to testify. It should be a clear categorical rule, despite outcome of the case, that the whims of the witness cannot in the balance between public and defendant interests, overshadow those two strong interests.

b. *interest in preserving state secrets*

This is a problem posed by the government's desire to use certain evidence against the criminal defendant to obtain a conviction, yet also desire to protect that same evidence from public disclosure because it is a state secret. In addition to the public's interest in obtaining conviction which it may in this instance sacrifice its interest in access to trial, the defendant has a right of discovery in most states and by federal law that will protect a defendant from a conviction based upon evidence essential to his defense that has been kept secret from him.[87] Once the evidence is admitted at trial, it becomes a part of the public record.

To protect the government's desired end, preservation of the secret, the court has to close the proceeding when the evidence is presented, grant defendant discovery on the condition that the evidence will not be released to the public, and then seal the record once the evidence is admitted at trial. These are serious restrictions upon the Sixth and First Amendments, even though the restrictions may well be justified in such cases as *U.S. v. Bell* [88] where anti-hijacking procedures were being discussed and its effectiveness would be lost if disclosed, but cannot be justified merely because undercover agents are involved in the case and are still active in the same community. Two recent New York court decisions[89] seem to agree with this view and reversed convictions because the only evidence to support closure in these narcotics trials was the prosecutor's statement as to the need to preserve the secrecy and safety of the undercover agents who were still active.

Therefore before restrictions of the First or Sixth Amendments can be imposed, it is not enough to merely narrowly draw such restrictions in either the witness' privacy cases or the state secrecy cases. Rather the court, particularly in the state secrecy cases should closely scrutinize the secret and determine how it may best remain effective in the continued prosecution of crime with the least amount of constitutional restriction. There are alternative ways of preserving the secrecy and the safety of not only undercover agents, but reluctant witnesses as well, such as having open trials, but camouflaging their faces,[90] thereby not lessening the effectiveness of the testimony or public access.

Part II - *Richmond Newspapers, Inc., v. Commonwealth of Virginia*: Has judicial access come into its own?

Much confusion reigned among the courts throughout the country about the meaning of *Gannett v. DePasquale*. In the wake of the decision in 1979 above, the Reporters Committee for Freedom of the Press cites 81 attempts at closure of which 48 were initially enforced or upheld on appeal. The number is only significant when one notes the breakdown of the types of criminal proceedings sought to be closed: 3 pre-indictment proceedings, 59 pretrial proceedings, 15 trials, and 4 post-trial hearings,[91] while remembering that *Gannett* concerned closure of a pretrial suppression hearing. Even the jury voir dire portion of a criminal trial was closed[92] in the name of *Gannett*.

In addition to the increases in closure of pretrial hearings and trials, press criticism was also widespread. Therefore, it is not surprising that the court would be faced with another opportunity to try it again on the issue of judicial access and to either clarify or abandon *Gannett*. It was given its opportunity in *Richmond Newspapers* and Chief Justice Burger wrote the 7 to 1 decision, though there were four concurring opinions, and Justice Powell took no part in the consideration of the case.

The case here involves the decision of a Virginia trial judge to close the trial pursuant to statute[93] on motion of defense counsel without objection by prosecution or by appellants, a newspaper and two of its reporters who were present in the courtroom at this the defendant's fourth trial on the same murder charge. In both the trial court and the Virginia Supreme Court, appellants argued that constitutional rights of the public and the press under the First Amendment prevented the court from closing a trial without first giving notice and an opportunity for a hearing to the public and the press and exhausting every alternative means of protecting the defendant's right to a fair trial.

In the majority opinion, Chief Justice Burger made clear that *Gannett* was not being abandoned or overturned. He clearly distinguishes *Gannett* by noticing that "the precise issue presented here (in *Richmond Newspapers*) has not previously been before this Court for decision."[94] He adheres in *Richmond Newspapers* to his position in *Gannett* that hearings on pretrial motions are to be distinguished from trials, and that the Court in *Gannett* decided on the Sixth Amendment public trial issue and did not decide the First Amendment issue.

Proving that history is always there to be used in whatever way one may need it, he used historical evidence to support his contention that even when our laws were adopted, criminal trials were presumptively open. Using the same evidence in *Gannett*, he found the exclusionary rule was not known at the writing of the Sixth Amendment and therefore not presumptively open to the public.

In his attempt to be consistent with the holding of *Pell* and *Saxbe*, though he recognized the public's right to attend criminal trials, he emphasizes that "(i)t is not crucial whether we describe this right to attend criminal trials .... as a 'right of access' or a 'right to gather information.'...."[95] He seems to clearly signal to the press that it is getting no fat, only lean. It also seems clear that he is adhering to his "equal access" rule and that total exclusion of public and press is okay in penal institutions, but not trials, because penal institutions .... by definition, are not 'open' or public places ....(and).... do not share the long tradition of openness, although there have been visiting committees of citizens, and .... 'visitation rights...'"[96]

Relying upon the First Amendment freedoms of speech, press and assembly (public-forum argument), and the Ninth Amendment[97] "unarticulated implicit rights" for those who argue the Constitution nowhere spells out a right to attend criminal trials in implicit in the guarantees of the First Amendment,"[98] and parenthetically by footnote adds, though the question of civil cases was not raised, that "historically both civil and criminal trials have been presumptively open."[99]

Like most categorical rules on First Amendment guarantees, the right to attend criminal trials is not absolute[100] and closure has not been placed alongside prior restraint in the constitutionally impermissible category. Rather by highlighting the Virginia judge's errors, Chief Justice Burger proscribed procedural implementation of his rule in the event some reasonable limitations on access to trial need be imposed: make findings to support closure; make an inquiry as to whether alternative solutions would meet the need to insure fairness; recognize the constitutional public and press right to attend (by giving them notice of closure and an opportunity to be heard, *Gannett*, *Westchester*).

Justice White, a dissenter in *Gannett*, felt that had the Sixth Amendment been properly construed as a public interest and not solely a personal right of the accused, there would not have been a need for the First Amendment to be addressed.[101] In light of the need for substantive development of the First Amendment, particularly in the area of access, if *Gannett* forced this First Amendment decision, then it was a blessing in disguise.

While Justice Steven's jubilation in this decision is understandable in light of his dissent in *Houchins* in favor of constitutional recognition of a right of access to public facilities without arbitrary governmental interference, his calling this a "watershed case" may be true because of the projected direction the Court may be heading on subsequent access issues, but may not be true of the embrace of the "acquisition of newsworthy matter" issue. He states that "never before has (the Court) squarely held that the acquisition of newsworthy matter is entitled to any constitutional protection whatsoever."[102] However, in light of Chief Justice Burger's express refusal to embrace the concepts of the "right of access" or the "right to gather information", except for his reiterated embrace of the *Branzburg* phrase that "without some protection for seeking out the news, freedom of the press could be eviscerated,"[103] it is unclear just how "squarely the Court so held." Chief Justice Burger's embrace of the *Branzburg* "some protection for seeking out the news" position is not very comforting considering the phrase was embraced every time access was denied or restricted in *Pell*, *Saxbe* and *Houchins* on the basis of the *Branzburg* majority's qualified recognition of newsgathering with limitations as to certain places.

The only other indication that the majority opinion written by Chief Justice Burger may be taking the position advocated by Justice Stevens is a vague footnote that says:

> The Constitution guarantees more than simply freedom from those abuses which led the Framers to single out particular rights. *The very purpose of the First Amendment is to guarantee all facets of each right described*; its draftsmen sought both to protect the "rights of Englishmen" and to enlarge their scope.[104]

This is a broad, as well as a vague, passage that may well signal Chief Justice Burger's intent to "enlarge the scope of First Amendment rights," but it is an intent that we will have to look for in subsequent cases. Perhaps it can be argued that this passage *implicitly* embraces the constitutional right of acquisition of newsworthy matter as an extension of the press clause. However, explicitly the majority decision seems to be as consistently focusing upon the right of attendance based upon the place, rather than the information to be derived therefrom, as it was in the prison access cases.

Justice Stevens further

> thought it ironic that the Court should find more reason to recognize a right of access (in *Richmond*) than it did in *Houchins*, involv(ing) the plight of a segment of society least able to protect itself, an attack on a long-standing policy of concealment, and an absence of any legitimate justification for abridging public access to information about how government operates.[105]

Yet though it is ironic, it is completely consistent based upon the theoretical methodology used in deciding both cases. In both instances, the majority approach was to look at the legal quality of the activity sought and determine whether that activity was constitutionally protected. Upon determining the legal quality of the activity, categorical rules were formulated: access to prisons by the press for newsgathering is not constitutionally protected, but access to *trials* by the press and the public for newsgathering is constitutionally protected. Stevens and the dissenters in *Houchins*, *Pell* and *Saxbe* part ways from the beginning of the legal query: whether the activity is constitutionally protected or not. Once the dissenters determine the activity is protected, they then look at the facts, plug them into a balancing test and determine the outcome accordingly. Therefore, the irony between the two cases is how the same methodology can produce such differing results.

Justice Brennan, joined by Justice Marshall notes that "the First Amendment has not been viewed by the Court in all settings as providing an equally categorical assurance of the correlative freedom of access of information.[106] Brennan advocates that the "resolution of First Amendment public access claims in individual cases must be strongly influenced by the weight of historical practice and by an assessment of the specific structural value of public access in the circumstances.[107] Applying this balancing approach to this case, he weighed the historical and current practice with respect to open trials against the importance of public access to the trial process itself and concluded that the "ingrained tradition of public trials and the importance of public access to the broader purposes of the trial process,[108] tip the balance strongly toward the rule that trials be open."[109]

Of course the foundation of Brennan's argument is his adoption of the societal function of the press to inform the public. Therefore he does not have to, as does Chief Justice Burger, "invoke a veritable potpourri of (constitutional sources), and a cluster of penumbral guarantees recognized in past decisions"[110] to find a First Amendment public interest to balance against the trial process. His approach producing a workable, general standard to the substantive development of First Amendment guarantees in a way Chief Justice Burger's categorical approach particularly where narrowly construed, will not.

Relying upon the "public-forum" argument, Justice Stewart in his concurring opinion, concluded because "a trial is by very definition a proceeding open to the press and to the public, the First and Fourteenth clearly give the press and the public a right of access to trials themselves, civil as well as criminal."[111] Furthering with the logical progression of that argument, he adds, "(j)ust as a legislature may impose reasonable time, place and manner restrictions upon the exercise of First Amendment freedoms, so may a trial judge impose reasonable limitations upon the unrestricted occupation of a courtroom by representatives of the press and members of the public."[112]

Justice Stewart has openly extended the First Amendment right of access to civil trials, while the majority opinion, recognizing the issue posed was a criminal trial, only implied by footnote that civil may also be subject to this right of access. His reliance, like all the other similar opinions on the historical openness of trials to support his public-forum argument to develop his categorical rule has the limitation that only traditionally open forums would satisfy the argument. Therefore the balancing approach promulgated by *Gayned* affords greater adaptability, though less certainty as to the outcome. *Gayned*, like Justice Brennan's approach, would look at the *effect* of the access upon the facility to make the determination and not rely solely upon the characterization of the facility as traditionally public or not.

Justice Blackmun's greatest contribution in concurring in this decision is to highlight a flaw of this decision and all of the opinions, including his own: the right to attend criminal trials has been eschewed, but without a clear standard of closure. By observing "that uncertainty marks the nature - and strictness - of the standard of closure the Court adopts,"[113] he recites the various standards mentioned by the Justices:

> The plurality opinion speaks of "an overriding interest articulated in findings,"....; Mr. Justice Steward reserves, perhaps not inappropriately, "reasonable limitations,"....; Mr. Justice Brennan presents his separate analytical framework; Mr. Justice Powell in *Gannett* was critical of those Justices who, relying on the Sixth Amendment, concluded that closure is authorized only when "strictly and inescapably necessary,"....; and Mr. Justice Rehnquist continues his flat rejection, of, among others, the First Amendment route. [114]

With that observation, he falls into the same trap. He promulgated the rule that the "right to a public trial is to be found where the Constitution explicitly placed it - in the

Sixth Amendment,"[115] by his position in *Gannett*, and unless by implication by his remark about the propriety of Justice Stewart's "reasonable limitations" standard, he promulgated no standard of his own. He only secondarily supports the First Amendment provision for public access to trial, only so as to reach the result that the judge erred by closing the trial in Virginia.

Though he is correct that a certain and strict standard for closure has emerged from this decision, it can be read to require a procedure for courts to have to follow that would eliminate summary closure based upon either agreement of counsel or motions from either side supported by mere verbal assertions of facts. The procedure would require a hearing so that there could be "findings" as to the need for closure, whereupon the judge would consider the least restrictive means necessary to accomodate that need for closure and then impose "reasonable limitations." Of course, trial judges will only know after appeal whether their "findings" were overriding enough to warrant the limitations they imposed. Since there are no guidelines, trial judges will be acting within the scope of their discretion as to the weight of the findings, and unless way out of line and heavy-handed, they will not likely be overturned.

Justice Rehnquist is as adamant as he was in *Gannett* that where both the prosecuting attorney and the defendant have consented to an order of closure approved by the judge that the matter is not subject to constitutional review. He believes that neither the First or Sixth Amendments and particularly not the Ninth Amendment "confers upon (the Court) any power to review orders of state trial judges closing trials in such situations"[116] and that the Court has no business interfering.

It is an error to believe that the United States Supreme Court has no responsibility for the proper administration of justice. It is proper for the sole interpreter of the U.S. Constitution to "rein in, as this Court has done over the past generation, all of the ultimate decision-making power over how justice shall be administered,"[117] so as to insure that the justice that is administered in the federal system and the 50 states is done so by the same *constitutional* standard. It is one of the few ways we can begin to believe that there can be justice for all.

Part III - Conclusion

In the development of First Amendment rights and judicial proceedings there are a few truisms: where the press is perceived as an institution, abridgment of the right to publish and disseminate information will not be tolerated by law or by judicial order, and virtual absolute First Amendment protection is accorded. The other truism is that where the scope of the First Amendment press clause has to be expanded beyond the right to publish and disseminate to the right to acquire information without infringement from law or judicial order, so as to inform the public, virtual absolute First Amendment protection is not accorded, due to other competing societal interests.

The judicial doctrine on First Amendment content and dissemination issues is clear and consistent. The judicial doctrine on First Amendment right of access to information is unclear, but young in development, particularly access to judicial proceedings. Therefore, the two principle judicial access cases - *Gannett* and *Richmond Newspapers* - are in the forefront of the development of judicial doctrine in this a rea of First Amendment law.

For those who criticized *Gannett* as an anomaly must note its survival in *Richmond Newspapers* and whether it will subsequently be eroded remains to be seen. Though the plurality opinions in both of these took a categorical approach in promulgating the rules of access, the future issues to be raised in this judicial access area will likely be resolved by the balancing approaches discussed in the concurring opinions; Justice Powell's opinion in *Gannett* and especially Justice Brennan's approach in *Richmond Newspapers*. In anticipating subsequent issues to be raised, Justice Brennan has already tipped his hand using his analytical approach when he concluded that bench interchanges and conferences in chambers were distinct from trial proceedings and not subject to public or press intrusion.[118] The resolution of the interpretation of the press clause conflict among the Justices themselves will probably do most to cement the judicial doctrine of the First Amendment right of access to information. If indeed the majority in *Richmond Newspapers* held squarely that there is a constitutional right of acquisition of newsworthy material, as Justice Stevens asserts, then that would be a signal of a meeting of the minds among the Justices on the societal function of the press. Our modern society today and its dependence upon the media requires no less. The real glimmer of hope is Chief Justice Burger's footnoted remark that "the very purpose of the First Amendment is to guarantee *all facets of each right described* .... *and to enlarge their scope*."[119] (Emphasis added.) The ramifications of this statement are most encouraging in the development of substance of the First Amendment guarantees, and particularly encouraging for subsequent cases that raise the issue squarely: is there a right of acquisition of newsworthy matter.

With the rules having now been promulgated on the basic right of access to judicial proceedings, subsequent judicial access cases will redefine the questions of what "reasonable limitations" imposed upon access are and of what findings are sufficient to constitute "overriding interests" supporting closure. It is strongly recommended that in this refinement process, theories such as "equal access" and "public-forum" yield for more of an analytical framework that will require subliminal and not just surface investigation.

[1] *Bridges v. California*, 314 U.S. 252 (1941).

[2] *Pennekamp v. Florida*, 328 U.S. 331 (1946) and *Craig v. Harney*, 331 U.S. 375 (1961).

[3] *Wood v. Georgia*, 370 U.S. 375 (1961).

[4] *Landmark Communications, Inc. v. Virginia*, 435 U.S. 829 (1978).

[5] *Hague v. C.I.O.*, 307 U.S. 496, 515 (1939); *Schneider v. State*, 308 U.S. 147 (1938); *Cox v. New Hampshire*, 312 U.S. 569 (1941); and *Jamison v. Texas*, 318 U.S. 413 (1943). These cases constitute a reversal of the *Commonwealth v. Davis*, 162 Mass. 510 (1895) dictum that public property did not belong to the public for use, but instead belonged to the state. See also, Stoney, G., "Fora American: Speech in Public Places," 1974 *Sup. Ct. Rev.* 233, 237.

[6] *Edwards v. South Carolina*, 372 U.S. 229 (1963).

[7] *Adderley v. Florida*, 385 U.S. 39 (1966).

[8] 408 U.S. 104 (1972).

[9] 408 U.S. at 116-117.

[10] 48 U.S.L.W. 5008 (1980).

[11] 49 U.S.L.W. 4141 (1981).

[12] 333 U.S. 257 (1947).

[13] 333 U.S. at 268.

[14] 333 U.S. at 269.

[15] *Id.* at 270.

[16] *Lacraze v. U.S.*, 391 F. 2d 516 (5th Cir., 1968).

[17] *Richmond Newspapers*, *supra* at note 1, *Id* at 5012, footnote.

[18] Note, "Trial Secrecy and the First Amendment Right of Public Access to Judicial Proceedings," 91 *Harv. L. Rev.* 1899, 1912 (1978).

[19] *In re Oliver*, *Id* at 271-272; *U.S. v. Kobli*, 172 F. 2d 919 (1949).

[20] *Illinois v. Allen*, 397 U.S. 337 (1970).

[21] See, e.g., *Estes v. Texas*, 381 U.S. 532 (1965).

[22] See, footnote 18, Id.

[23] 384 U.S. 333, 335 (1966).

[24] 384 U.S. at 357.

[25] *Id.*

[26] 384 U.S. at 363.

[27] 384 U.S. at 360-361 and 363.

[28] 384 U.S. at 358.

[29] 381 U.S. 532 (1965).

[30] 381 U.S. at 533.

[31] Broholm, J.R., "Electronic Media in the Courtroom," *Case and Comment*, Vol. 85, No 3 (May-June, 1980), p. 10.

[32] Broholm, Id at 9, citing Judith L. Kreeger, "Cameras in the Courtroom," 52 *Florida Bar Journal*, 451-2 (June, 1978).

[33] To overcome the fear that television would degrade the dignity of judicial proceedings by commercial interruptions, by selectively presenting only the entertaining portions of trials, by hyping up the interest in the trial by over-dramatic commentary or making it look like a game and by converting the participants into television-digestible caricatures, Chief Justice Warren suggested that television networks "might provide expert commentary on the proceedings and hire persons with legal backgrounds to anticipate possible trial strategy, as the football expert anticipates plays for his audience." 381 U.S. at 572.

[34] Note, 91 *Harv. L. Rev.*, at 1912.

[35] *Id* at 5015, footnote.

[36] Note, 91 *Harv. L. Rev.* at 1914.

[37] 443 U.S. 382, 99 S. Ct. 2898, 61 L. Ed. 2d 608 (1979).

[38] 51 L.Ed. 2d at 633.

[39] 427 U.S. 539 (1976).

[40] 343 U.S. 181 (1952).

[41] 369 U.S. 541 (1962).

[42] 421 U.S. 794 (1975).

[43] 427 U.S. at 554.

[44] Schmidt, *supra* at note 2, *Id* at 445.

[45] ABA Advisory Committee on Fair Trial and Free Press, headed by Justice Paul C. Reardon of the Massachusetts Supreme Judicial Court Reardon Report (1968) adopted as part of the ABA's *Standards for Criminal Justice* research by lawyers. Research studies by social scientists: The Chicago Jury Study by Kalven and Zeisel, *The American Jury* (1966); Tans and Chaffee, "Pretrial Publicity and Juror Prejudice," 43 *Journalism Q* 647 (1966); Wilcox and McCombs, "Crime Story Elements and Fair Trial/Free Press" in Wilcox, "The Press, the Jury and the Behavioral Sciences," 9 *Journalism Monographs* 20 (1968); Simon, "Murder, Juries and the Press," 3 Trans-Action 40 (May-June, 1966); Kline and Jess, "Prejudicial Publicity; Its Effects on Law School Mock Juries," 43 *Journalism Q* 113 (1966); Padawar-Singer and Barton, "The Impact of Pretrial Publicity on Juror's Verdicts," in The Jury System in America (R. Simon ed. 1975) and Simon and Eimermann, "The Jury Finds Not Guilty: Another Look at Media Influence on the Jury," 48 *Journalism Q* 343 (1971) all cited in Simon, R., "Does the Court's Decision in *Nebraska Press Association* Fit the Research Evidence on the Impact on Jurors

of News Coverage?" 29 *Stanford L. Rev.* 515 (1977).

[46] See note 45.

[47] See note 45, *Id* at 32, cited in Schmidt, *Id* at 447.

[48] 427 U.S. at 559.

[49] 427 U.S. at 562.

[50] Goodale, James C., "Open Justice: The Threat of *Gannett*," 1 *Communications and the Law* 3, 9 (1979).

[51] 427 U.S. at 563.

[52] Goodale, *Id*.

[53] *New York Times Co. v. United States* 403 U.S. 713 (1971).

[54] *Landmark Communications*, supra.

[55] 427 U.S. at 556.

[56] 283 U.S. 697 (1931).

[57] Denying access to information is equivalent to denying the right to disseminate the information *only* if the prospective disseminator is entitled to possess the information in the first instance. See, e.g., *CBS, Inc. v. Young*, 522 F 2d 234 (6th Cir., 1975). *In the courtroom situation, this means that closure cannot be considered a prior restraint unless an antecedent*

- 47 -

right of attendance has been recognized. (Emphasis added.) Note, "The Right to Attend Criminal Hearings," 78 *Columbia L. Rev.*, 1308, 1317-1318 (1978).

[58] 427 U.S. at 568.

[59] 424 N.Y.S. 2d 972 (N.Y. Sup. Ct., 1980).

[60] 424 N.Y.S. 2d at 974.

[61] 424 N.Y.S. at 975.

[62] *Westchester Rockland Newspapers v. Leggett*, 48 N.Y. 2d 430, 423 N.Y.S. 2d 630, 399 N.E. 2d 518 (1979) Procedural guidelines to be followed by counsel and the courts where a pretrial court proceeding closure is sought: (1) a motion must be made in open court; (2) there must be the demonstration of a "strong likelihood of prejudice; and (3) there must be the making of a record and the expression by the court of its reason for closure.

[63] 423 N.Y.S. 2d at 438.

[64] 424 N.Y.S. 2d at 978.

[65] 589 P. 2d 322 (Wyo, 1979).

[66] 607 P. 2d 1259 (Wyo, 1980).

[67] Where a record is not established, is unclear or incomplete, as where statement by either counsel is the lone basis for closure, courts have consistently not upheld the closure order. See, e.g., *Gannett Pa-*

- 48 -

cIfic Corp v. Richardson, 580 P. 2d 49 (1978).

[68] 431 F. Supp 1182, aff'd 556 F. 2d 706 (4th Cir, 1977), cert. denied 54 L.Ed 2d 771, 98 S. Ct. 749 (1978).

[69] Where there has been support for the press' right of newsgathering, the Court has gone the other way on this issue. In *CBS, Inc. v. Young*, 522 F 2d 234 (6th Cir., 1975) (per curiam), the Court held that a gag order entered against participants in a publicized trial constituted a prior restraint on petitioner CBS (Columbia Broadcasting Service), even though CBS was not subject to the order. To reach this conclusion, the court had to find that CBS had standing to bring the suit. It therefore found that CBS had standing because it had a protected right to gather information from those trial participants who were willing to speak to CBS. By having an entitlement to their information, the gag order injured CBS by infringing upon its right to receive information from a willing source. *Id* at 237-238.

[70] Given the possible consequences of a trial participants' violation of the court's gag order, contempt of court, one would think that if a trial participant objected on the basis of a prior restraint upon speech that the clear and present danger test would apply. However, the same "reasonably likely" test was applied in *People v. Dupree*, 388 N.Y.S. 2d 203 (1976) where a defense lawyer challenged the gag order on First Amendment

grounds and in *U.S. v. Tijerina*, 412 F. 2d 661 (10th Cir., 1969), cert. denied 396 U.S. 990 (1969) where the court upheld the contempt violations of two defendants who had violated the court's order barring extrajudicial statements prior to trial. In *Leach v. Sawicki*, 46 U.S.L.W. 3377 (Dec. 6, 1977) cert. denied, 48 U.S.L.W. 3436 (Jan. 10, 1978) which involved an unreported order of the Ohio Supreme Court, witnesses, jurors and lawyers were forbidden to talk to the press "without any finding of a clear and present danger to the trial or even a reasonable likelihood of such danger, ... the court may have applied no test whatsoever in restraining speech." Goodale, *supra*, *Id* at 10, footnote 29.

[71] *Chicago Council of Lawyers v. Bauer*, 522 F. 2d 242 (7th Cir., 1975), cert. denied, 427 U.S. 912.

[72] 47 N.Y. 2d 985, 419 N.Y.S. 2d 965, 393 N.E. 2d 1038 (1979).

[73] Note, *supra* at 91, *Id* at 1311, quoting Fenner and Koley, "The Rights of the Press and the Closed Court Criminal Proceeding," 57 *Neb. L. Rev.* 442, 454 (1978); and *State ex rel Dayton Newspaper, Inc. v. Phillips*, 46 Ohio St. 2d 457, 471, 351 N.E. 2d 127, 136 (1976)(Stern, J., concurring).

[74] *Sheppard*, *Id* at 358.

[75] 435 U.S. 589 (1978).

[76] 420 U.S. 469 (1975).

[77] 435 U.S. at 609.

[78] 435 U.S. at 606.

[79] 558 F. 2d 1202 (5th Cir., 1977).

[80] 558 F. 2d at 1208.

[81] 558 F. 2d at 1209.

[82] Justice William J. Brennan Address, 32 *Rutegers Law Rev.*, 173, 177 (1979).

[83] *United States ex rel Latimore v. Sielaff*, 561 F. 2d 691, (7th Cir., 1977).

[84] *United States ex rel Smallwood v. Lavalle*, 377 F. Supp. 1148 (E.D.N.Y., 1974).

[85] *Kirstowsky v. Superior Court of Sonoma County*, 143 Cal. App. 2d 745, 300 P. 2d 163 (1956).

[86] *Geise v. United States*, 262 F. 2d 151 (9th Cir., 1958).

[87] *Rovario v. United States*, 353 U.S. 53, 60-61 (1957) and *Jencks v. United States*, 353 U.S. 657, 672 (1957). 262 F. 2d 151 (9th Cir., 1958).

[88] 464 F. 2d 667 (2d Cir.), cert. denied 409 U.S. 991 (1972).

[89] *People v. Cousart*, 426 N.Y.S. 2d 295 (N.Y.A.D., 1980) and *People v. Gonzalez*, 426 N.Y.S. 2d 318 (N.Y.A.D., 1980).

[90] Technique suggested in *CBS, Inc. v. Superior Court*, 85 Cal. App. 3rd 241, 149 Cal. Rptr. 421 (1978) where defendant's right to discovery of film footage of undercover agents was in conflict with First Amendment right of "news gathering."

[91] 48 L.W. 2382 (December 4, 1979).

[92] *Rapid City Journal Company v. Circuit Court of the Seventh Judicial Circuit*, 283 N.W. 2d 563 (S.D. Sup. Ct., 1979), although in most cases less reason exists to exclude the public from the voir dire than any other stage of the trial, the voir dire in this case was exceptional, because jurors were questioned concerning their religious affiliation, their views on abortion, and whether their views matched the views of their church.

[93] Virginia Closure Statute, Va. Code 19.2-266: "In the trial of all criminal cases, whether the same be felony or misdemeanor cases, the court, may in its discretion, exclude from the trial any persons whose presence would impair the conduct of a fair trial, provided that the right of the accused to a public trial shall note be violated." Appellants; Brief, p. 4.

[94] 48 L.W. at 5010.

[95] 48 L.W. 5013.

[96] 48 L.W. 5013, footnote 11.

[97] Fundamental rights, even though not ex-

pressly guaranteed, have been recognized by the Court as indispensable to the enjoyment of rights explicitly defined. For example, the rights of association and of privacy, the right to be presumed innocent and the right to be judged by a standard of proof beyond a reasonable doubt in a criminal trial, as well as the right to travel, appear nowhere in the Constitution or Bill of Rights. 48 L.W. at 5014.

[98] 48 L.W. 5015.

[99] *Id* at footnote 17.

[100] 48 L.W. at 5015, footnote 18: "We have no occasion here to define the circumstances in which all or parts of a criminal trial may be closed to the public, ... but our holding today does not mean that the First Amendment rights of public and representation of the press are absolute."

[101] (White, J., concurring) 48 L.W. at 5015.

[102] (Stevens, J., concurring) 48 L.W. at 5015.

[103] 408 U.S. at 681.

[104] 48 L.W. at 5014, footnote 14.

[105] (Stevens, J., concurring) 48 L.W. at 5015.

[106] (Brennan, J., concurring) 48 L.W. at 5016.

[107] (Brennan, J., concurring) 48 L.W. at 5019.

[108] To assure the criminal defendant a fair

and accurate adjudication of guilt or innocence; to satisfy the appearance of justice; to assure the public that procedural rights are respected and afforded equally; a checks and balance system akin to the other checks and balances that infuse our system of government; aids accurate fact-finding. 48 L.W. at 5018-5019.

[109] 48 L.W. at 5019.

[110] (Blackmun, J., concurring) 48 L.W. at 5021.

[111] (Stewart, J., concurring) 48 L.W. at 5020.

[112] *Id* at 5020.

[113] (Blackmun, J., concurring) 48 L.W. at 5021.

[114] *Id*.

[115] *Id* at 5021.

[116] (Rehnquist, J., dissenting) 48 L.W. at 5021.

[117] *Id*.

[118] (Brennan, J., concurring) 48 L.W. at 5019.

[*119*] *Op. cit*.

THE SUPREME COURT AND DEVELOPMENT OF FEDERAL HABEAS CORPUS DOCTRINE

The development of federal habeas corpus doctrine has followed an erratic course of expansion and contraction by both Congress and the Supreme Court. The Supreme Court's current inclination toward disengagement from earlier efforts to reform law enforcement (efforts symbolized by such decision as *Mapp* and *Miranda*) is reflected in part in its recent narrowing of habeas corpus jurisdiction.

Article III of the United States Constitution made no specific provision for the issuance of writs of habeas corpus. This writ, called by Jefferson the "great writ of liberty," was protected under Article I, Section 9 of the Constitution from infringement except in cases of rebellion, invasion, or threat to public safety.

The writ, meaning "having the body", is an instrument whereby a court can compel ministers of the state to produce an individual being incarcerated, and to show cause of committment. Habeas corpus, then, provides the judiciary with a means for keeping in check the executive's exercise of police powers.

Although dealt with in two pieces of legislation subsequent to the Constitution, and the subject of numerous United States Supreme Court decisions, the writ of habeas corpus remains very loosely defined and rests primarily on its English common law origins. The greatest importance of the writ of habeas corpus is that within the federal system of government it provides a means of collateral review - pursuing judicial relief in both the state and national court system. Thus, no matter what changes have occurred in federal habeas corpus jurisdiction, the writ has always been a potentially important means for the administration of justice.

The following review should not be taken as a complete listing of United States Supreme Court habeas corpus decisions. Neither will there be an extensive recitation of the essential, substantive aspects of the cases. Rather, this summary is intended to show the changing attitudes and policies of the Supreme Court in the area of review of state court decisions through application of the writ of habeas corpus.

Judiciary Act of 1789 to Close of the Civil War

One of the earliest United States Supreme Court cases arising under the habeas corpus provisions of the Judiciary Act of 1789 was that of *Ex parte Watkins*[1] Watkin's appeal, by writ of habeas corpus, was denied by the Supreme Court on the grounds that this method could not be used to circumvent the Court's lack of jurisdiction in criminal cases. Essentially the Court was being asked to use habeas corpus as an exercise of its appellate jurisdiction. The question was, could a petitioner appeal directly to the Supreme Court by means of habeas corpus? In rendering its decision, the Supreme Court held that the judgment of a federal court of appropriate jurisdiction could not be attacked by means of habeas corpus.

Early Reconstruction to the Warren Era

The Civil War brought on a sequence of habeas corpus beginning with *Ex parte Milligan*[2] Lambdin Milligan was charged with conspiracy, treason, and insurrection for plotting the freeing of Confederate prisoners held in Ohio and Indiana during the Civil War. Because of the nature of the charges, Milligan and his co-conspirators were tried before military tribunals rather than in the federal, civilian courts of Indiana. All of the defendants were found guilty and subsequently appealed their cases on writs of habeas corpus based on the lack of a jury trial. Justice Davis, in delivering the opinion for the Supreme Court, stated in sweeping language that the laws of war "can never be applied to citizens of states which have upheld the authority of the government, and where the courts are open and their process unobstructed."

Additionally, Justice Davis noted that there rightly existed a provision for the suspension of the writ of habeas corpus and that martial law could be properly utilized. He hastened to add, however, that "suspension of the privilege of the writ of habeas corpus does not suspend the writ itself."

One of the most significant Civil War-related cases was that of *Ex parte McCardle*[3] McCardle dealt with issues concerning military governments and trials. The Habeas Corpus Act of 1867 provided for appeals by prisoners held in violation of federal laws. Military prisoners were specifically excluded from these provisions, and as Tribe notes "....there is no Article III judicial review .... of most questions of law decided by military courts."[4]

Before the Supreme Court could rule on *McCardle*, and indirectly on the constitutionality of Reconstruction, Congress repealed the Habeas Corpus Act of 1867. Even though it was presumed that this would apply to future appeals, the Supreme Court ruled that the repeal removed its jurisdiction from the *McCardle* case.

Chief Justice Salmon P. Chase delivered the opinion for the Court in *McCardle*. Chase recognized that there was some question concerning the effect of the repeal of habeas corpus jurisdiction over cases filed prior to the repeal. However, he held that on two prior occasions the Supreme Court had ruled that "no judgment could be rendered in a suit after the repeal of the act under which it was brought and prosecuted."[5]

In the same year it heard *McCardle*, the Supreme Court decided *Ex parte Yerger*.[6] The *Yerger* case, like *McCardle*, dealt with a petitioner held in military custody. Also like *McCardle*, Yerger's petition for habeas corpus had been dismissed by the federal district court. However, unlike *McCardle*, Yerger did not base his appeal on the Habeas Corpus Act of 1867. His petition was based on the Supreme Court's habeas corpus jurisdiction granted under the Judiciary Act of 1789.

In its decision, the Supreme Court, for all intents and purposes, invalidated the Act of 1868 removing its habeas corpus review powers and relied on its review powers granted originally under the Judiciary Act of 1789. Even though Yerger was released from custody before the Court could rule, the tenets of the *Yerger* case were carried forward until 1885 when Congress reinstated the habeas corpus appeal route originated in 1867 and repealed in 1868.

In the case of *Ex parte Royall*,[7] the Supreme Court issued it potentially most expansive habeas corpus edict. Here the Court held that federal courts had the power to release state prisoners held unconstitutionally, even prior to trial. However, the Court ruled that "....ordinarily the federal court should stay its hand on habeas pending completion of the state proceedings."

The next major habeas corpus decision was that of *Frank v. Mangum*.[8] In this case the petitioner had been convicted in a Georgia court on a charge of murder. In a trial atmosphere with strong overtones of anti-Semitism and the imminent threat of a lynchmob, the jury could not help but return a verdict of guilty. At this point it became irrelevant whether the prisoner was in federal or state custody.[9] The primary criteria for federal review became whether an individual

> ...was convicted on a confession involuntarily extracted, whether he was denied the right to counsel, whether the jury was fairly selected, whether the evidence against him was obtained by unlawful search and seizure, and whether he was not allowed adequate facilities to seek a review.[10]

In short, the questions presented by *Frank v. Mangum* was whether habeas corpus review could be used by the Supreme Court as a means of reviewing a fair trial question from a state court.

Federalism decreased in importance as federal courts pre-empted state court decisions; thus, in *Moore v. Dempsey*,[11] the Supreme Court granted habeas corpus relief to a state prisoner in order to insure a "fair trial." Here the prisoner had been convicted and sentenced to death under the threat of mob action. This threat made the trial merely a formality.[12] Although this case closely paralleled *Frank v. Mangum*, the majority opinion of *Frank* was largely repudiated.

The period of time intervening between *Frank* and *Moore* saw a philosophical shift in the Supreme Court. Justice William Brennan, later in *Fay v. Noia*,[13] asserted that habeas corpus was not as important before 1916 as afterward since many appeals were taken to the Supreme Court by right on writs of error. However, with the increasing usage of the Court's discretionary jurisdiction, by writ of certiorari, habeas corpus increased in importance after *Moore v. Dempsey*.

In *Ex parte Hawk*,[14] the petitioner had been confined to the Nebraska State Penitentiary upon his conviction for murder. Hawk had unsuccessfully applied for habeas corpus relief both in federal and state courts and, thus, brought his appeal to the United States Supreme Court after previously being denied certiorari.

Hawk's basic contention was that the Nebraska Court had forced him to trial so rapidly that his right to the assistance of counsel in a capital case was impaired. He also asserted that knowingly perjured evidence was utilized by the prosecution at his trial. In hearing this case, the United States Supreme Court denied the petition for habeas corpus relief on the grounds that Hawk had not adequately exhausted the state remedies available to him.

Many Supreme Court observers believe that the case of *Brown v. Allen*,[15] afforded the Court the opportunity to clarify its habeas corpus jurisdiction. But, when the opinions were written, the Court had divided into four distinct groups. In this case a state defendant's habeas corpus appeal was dismissed, whereupon he petitioned the United States Supreme Court for review by way of a writ of certiorari. The Supreme Court denied certiorari and the case was appealed again, by writ of habeas corpus, to the federal district court. Each stage of the federal court system had decreed that the case did not merit further federal action meaning, in following this appeal route, the case had appeared twice before the United States Supreme Court. Justice Jackson's opinion held that allowing dual channels of appeal would "not only burden our own docket and harass the state authorities but it makes a prisoner's legitimate quest for federal justice an endurance contest."

The same year that *Brown v. Allen* was decided a new period of Supreme Court history began. Earl Warren became Chief Justice of the Supreme Court and held the position for sixteen years.

The Warren Era (1953-69)

The real period of interest during the Warren years is that of the early 1960s. Prior to this the Supreme Court's decisions, though tending in large part to expand habeas corpus review, were highly particularized. However, two

1963 cases marked a shift to a broader definition of habeas corpus review.

Townsend v. Sain,[16] questioned the voluntary confession guidelines previously articulated by the Supreme Court. Here the "police adminstered a drug to the defendant for purposes of relieving his drug withdrawal pains; the officers were (allegedly) unaware of its 'truth serum' qualities."[17] Given this situation it was highly unlikely that the resultant confession could have met the Supreme Court's voluntariness criterion.

Townsend was convicted of murder and sentenced to die. After he had exhausted all of his state remedies, he applied to the federal district court for habeas corpus relief alleging that he had been convicted on a confession obtained while he was under the influence of a "truth serum."

The United States Supreme Court, in an opinion written by Chief Justice Warren, ruled that the state courts and the federal district court erred in not establishing the voluntariness of this confession. Warren maintained that the federal courts were obliged to grant an evidentiary hearing because the facts of the case remained in dispute.

Chief Justice Warren clearly articulated his position with regard to state courts in saying that

> Even where the procedure employed does not violate the Constitution, if it appears to be seriously inadequate for the ascertainment of the truth, it is the federal judge's duty to disregard the state findings and take evidence anew.[18]

Although Warren supported federal court intervention, the final issue was not the merit of the habeas corpus petition, but rather the procedural error of the district court in not granting an evidentiary hearing. *Townsend v. Sain* did, however, lay the groundwork for the case that was to mark habeas corpus jurisdiction at its broadest.

Fay v. Noia,[19] delineated the Supreme Court's most expansive interpretation of federal habeas corpus supervision of state criminal proceedings. This decision established precedent whereby a state prisoner could by-pass exhausting state remedies. Tribe maintains that the *Fay* decision

> ...signaled the lack of respect by federal courts for state procedures and at least potentially encouraged litigants in state courts not to worry about whether they had complied with state rules.[20]

In approaching state procedures in this manner, the Supreme Court increased its pressure on state courts, thus reducing autonomy and increasing resistance.[21]

Noia had been convicted of a murder committed during a robbery, and was subsequently sentenced to life imprisonment. The evidence against Noia, and two co-defendants, consisted entirely of confessions. The two co-defendants were eventually released after appeals showed their confessions to be coerced.

Noia's writ of habeas corpus was denied by federal district court on the grounds that he failed to exhaust his state remedies. The United States Supreme Court, in an opinion written by Justice Brennan, overturned that dismissal. Brennan asserted that historically there has been "respectable common-law authority for the proposition that habeas (corpus) was available to remedy any king of governmental restraint contrary to fundamental law." Thus,

> ...it would appear that the Constitution invites, if it does not compel .... a generous construction of the power of the federal courts to dispense the writ conformably with common-law practices.[22]

Brennan maintained that considerations of federalism no longer governed in cases such as this since the Judiciary Act of 1867 and subsequent federal statutes had extended federal habeas corpus jurisdiction to state prisoners. Thus, Flanders and Goldman summarize the impact of *Fay v. Noia* by saying that "as a result of the Supreme Court's decision .... procedural hurdles for state prisoners seeking post-conviction relief were dramatically reduced.[23]

The Post-Warren Era

If the cases of *Townsend v. Sain* and *Fay v. Noia* exemplify the Warren Court's approach to the question of habeas corpus jurisdiction, then *Francis v. Henderson*,[24] and *Stone v. Powell*,[25] provide similar boundary markers for the Burger Court.

In *Francis*, the petitioner, who had been convicted of murder, appealed his conviction after six years imprisonment on the grounds that the grand jury that indicted him was illegally constituted - that is, grand jury impanelment had systematically excluded Negroes from service. The Supreme Court held that habeas corpus was an appropriate avenue by which to seek relief, but the petitioner had failed to make a "timely challenge" to his conviction.

Justice Stewart held that the doctrines of comity and federalism require the same considerations for overturning state convictions as are required for overturning federal convictions. Thus, the petitioner would be required to show not only that the grand jury was illegally constituted, but also that this composition actually worked to his detriment.

It becomes apparent, then, that the Burger Court has moved away from the expansive interpretation represented by the Warren Court decisions of *Townsend v. Sain* and *Fay v. Noia*. This movement, although basically incremental, gained in momentum during the mid-1970s and reached its zenith with the decision of *Stone v. Powell*.

Conclusions

Expansion of the Supreme Court's habeas corpus jurisdiction proceeded slowly from the Judiciary Act of 1789 until the 1960s. Rulings originating with the Habeas Corpus Act of 1867 generally expanded the Supreme Court's supervisory power over state criminal procedure cases, but the greatest proliferation in the criminal segment of appellate activity began with the *Mapp* decision.[26] As a result of the Warren Court's receptiveness to the appeals of criminal defendants, the number of petitions for federal habeas corpus relief filed by state prisoners increased from 541 in 1952 to 7500 in 1969.[27]

The reversal of the trend toward expansion of habeas corpus jurisdiction has not come quickly, and decisions like *Francis v. Henderson* should not be viewed as ends in themselves, but rather as building blocks in the Burger Court's search for a new judicial federalism. If any one case could be considered the Burger Court's capstone, relative to issues of criminal procedure and attitudes toward federalism, it would be the case of *Stone v. Powell*.

Legal scholars point to *Stone v. Powell* as an obvious "retrenchment" by the Burger Court in the area of criminal procedure. Those individuals who have supported the expansive view of habeas corpus expounded during the Warren era maintain that *Stone v. Powell* erased decisions like *Fay v. Noia* going back more than a decade. Some have even suggested that the case destroys the stability of well-established criminal procedure and even impliedly overrules *Mapp v. Ohio*.

Finally, federal collateral attack, by way of habeas corpus review, has provided federal courts, especially the Supreme Court, with a powerful tool for monitoring state criminal procedure cases. Both Congress and the United States Supreme Court have occasionally broadened the sweep of federal review to provide closer scrutiny of state cases.

Whether the Burger Court is currently engaged in a period of entrenchment is still subject to debate. However, it seems apparent that in the area of criminal procedure the Burger Court is much less interventionist than was the Warren Court. On this point the Warren Court may prove to be the aberrant case, leaving the Burger Court to occupy a more traditional role in terms of judicial federalism and federal collateral review. Thus, a look at the development of federal habeas corpus doctrine provides valuable insight into the place of the Supreme Court in the criminal justice system, its relation to other courts, and its role in the historical evolution of habeas corpus review.

[1] 28 U.S. 193 (1830).

[2] 4 Wall. 2 (1866).

[3] 7 Wall. 506 (1869).

[4] Tribe, Laurence H., *American Constitutional Law* (Mineola, N.Y.: Foundation Press, 1978), p. 43.

[5] 7 Wall. 514.

[6] 8 Wall. 85 (1868).

[7] 117 U.S. (1886).

[8] 237 U.S. 314 (1915).

[9] Fairman, Charles. *History of the United States Supreme Court: Reconstruction and Reunion 1864-88.* (New York: MacMillan Co., 1971), p. 1426.

[10] Ibid.

[11] 261 U.S. 86 (1923).

[12] Gunther, Gerald. *Cases and Materials on Constitutional Law* (Mineola, N.Y.: Foundation Press, 1975), p. 511.

[13] 372 U.S. 413 (1963).

[14] 321 U.S. 114 (1944).

[15] 344 U.S. 443 (1953).

[16] 372 U.S. 293 (1963).

[17] Miller, Frank; Dawson, Robert; Dix, George; and Parnas, Raymond, *Cases and Materials in Criminal Justice Administration*. (Mineola, N.Y.: Foundation Press, 1976), p. 639.

[18] 372 U.S. 316.

[*19*] 372 U.S. 391 (1963).

[20] Tribe, *American Constitutional Law*, p. 128.

[21] Ibid., p. 129.

[22] 372 U.S. 406.

[23] Flanders, Steven and Goldman, Jerry, "Screening Practices and the Use of Para-Judicial Personnell in a U.S. Court of Appeals," in *Judicial Administration: Text and Readings*, eds. Russell R. Wheeler and Howard R. Whitcomb (Englewood Cliffs, N.J.: Prentice-Hall, 1977), p. 246.

[*24*] 425 U.S. 536 (1976).

[*25*] 428 U.S. 465 (1976).

[26] 367 U.S. 643 (1961).

[27] Warr, Paul. "Federal Habeas Corpus Review: Alive or Awake? *Journal of Contemporary Law* 3 (1977): 331.

PRE-TRIAL DIVERSION:
CONTINUING CONSTITUTIONAL CONCERNS

As court dockets become increasingly back-logged and as jails and prisons become more and more overcrowded, more attention should perhaps be focused on the tendency in American criminal law to overcriminalize the conduct of individuals. Overcriminalization, in turn, has caused enormous court caseloads - a situation which has led some courts to dismiss cases for evidentiary and due process reasons, although said disputes between involved parties continue to exist.[1] Other courts have found the accused guilty, but without the means to provide appropriate remedies - thus, rendering judgments *meaningless*.[2] Without doubt, such decisions reflect negatively on our methods of solving problems in the criminal justice system.

Pretrial diversion has been, in part, a response to overcriminalization. Variations of diversion have been proposed and implemented in the various states in search of better ways or alternatives in handling misdemeanor type controversies.[3] Such pretrial programs, unlike traditional pretrial intervention, do not require an admission of guilt. In fact, no presumption of guilt is made a condition of participating therein - it is an option voluntarily entered into by said parties.

Pretrial programs which have emphasized alternatives from the increased use of summons and citations in certain cases, entering into mediation and/or arbitration in other cases, and increased utilization of restitution are all creative resolutions in lieu of prosecution via the conventional criminal process.[4]

A typical program using the mediation/arbitration approach would handle selected complaints filed by aggrieved parties resulting in the issuance of a warrant for the arrest of a defendant for minor criminal offenses such as destruction of property, simple assault or harrassment.

Upon reviewing the complaints, the program is explained to the complainant. If the complainant desires to submit the case to arbitration/mediation and the submission is agreed to by the defendant and the District Attorney, and Mediation/Arbitration Program handles the case. The parties or their attorneys are able to introduce evidence, call witnesses and cross-examine witnesses during the proceedings. The parties are also informed that the award of the Arbitrator/Mediator is final, binding and enforceable.

Although many of the creative alternative approaches minimize the legal questions associated with compulsory guilty plea requirements inherent in participation in traditional pretrial intervention programs, other legal issues concerning Fourteenth Amendment due process safeguards and equal protection continue to exist in the administration of alternative programs.

Analysis of the pretrial diversion concept initially yields a well-intended and fair alternative to prosecution with a number of resulting advantages for the accused:

    a. Since the pretrial diversion agreement is not a conviction, the accused may give a negative reply on employment applications and similar forms when asked if (s)he has ever been convicted of an offense.

b. There is no public hearing with the resulting embarassment.

c. Diversion is less time consuming (when compared with movement of cases in court).

d. Participation frees the accused from pretrial detention and allows him the basic freedom of movement in the community.[5]

Yet, there are aspects of the various pretrial diversion programs about which we should be concerned.

In those states having diversion statutes, there are very few specific standards to guide administrators of such programs in deciding whether an individual has successfully completed diversion or whether his/her diversion status should be revoked and original charges reinstated. Also, by statute, prosecutors have great discretion in deciding which persons are admitted to state-operated diversion programs.

Since it appears that diversion programs in general do not offer minimal procedural guarantees, a divertee may have little or no recourse from later administrative decisions once (s)he begins to participate in a diversion program.

While the idea of diversion is well-intended and perhaps represents a fair alternative, legal questions continue to emerge from diversion situations as they affect the accused. Specific legal issues raised in recent cases in this area include:

a. Whether the due process clause of the Fourteenth Amendment entitles a pretrial divertee to an evidentiary hearing upon revocation of his/her diversionary status.

b. Whether a potential participant can (or should) be required to enter a formal plea of guilty as a prerequisite to being enrolled in a diversion program.

c. Whether there is a right to counsel in diversion revocation hearings.

d. Whether current procedures may infringe upon constitutional rights of the accused.

e. Whether the criteria, as stated and as applied, for eligibility amount to "arbitrary or capricious" deprivation or withdrawal of protected interests.

A number of state level cases coming from the New Jersey Supreme Court are illustrative of the emerging legal concerns in this area.

Three separate appeals concerning certain aspects of pretrial diversion programs were combined in the case of *New Jersey v. Leonardis*, (*Leonardis I*).[6] Two defendants, Leonardis and Rose, charged with offenses involving possession of controlled dangerous substances, filed actions for review when they were denied admission to a state operated pretrial diversion program. Under these criteria, the sale of a controlled dangerous substance constitutes a "heinous offense" and persons charged with such an offense are excluded from participation in pretrial diversion.

Both Leonardis and Rose were therefore denied admission to a state operated pretrial diversion program. Prosecutorial denials in these cases were based on exlusionary criteria as established by the Bergen County program.[7] Under these criteria, the sale of a controlled dangerous substance constitutes a "heinous offense" and persons charged with such an offense are excluded from participation in diversion.

Both Leonardis and Rose were therefore denied admission in accordance with program guidelines. Each defendant filed separate motions for the court to order the Director of the program to accept their applications. The reviewing trial judge denied motions of both defendants, reasoning that:

> Our decision rests on more fundamental deficiencies which we find inherent in the Bergen County PTI program and in its exclusionary criteria. Initially, we note that there was no malevolence on the part of the Bergen Courty program in adopting or administering these exclusionary criteria. Our conclusions are rather based upon the statewide experience with PTI and upon our desire to expand pretrial intervention beyond the programs (such as that in Bergen County) which pioneered the concept. Thus our observations are intended to apply to other PTI programs in New Jersey which exhibit the same deficiencies which we now consider.
>
> Our basic criticism of the Bergen County exclusionary criteria concerns the unduly restrictive impact which they may have on admissions in the program. In this regard, the criteria are inconsistent with the underlying liberal policy of R. 3:28. As a recent proposal for a

uniform, statewide PTI program states:
"New Jersey's R. 3:28 contains no criteria limiting participation to any class
of defendants, and although New Jersey
programs use guidelines for exclusion,
the guidelines show only those cases that
are ordinarily excluded. Enrollment
then, of the 'offender rather than the
offense' is the rule in New Jersey and
appears to be the trend of development
among programs nationally.[8]

Subsequent motions to the Appellate Division
were unsuccessful.

Thereafter, the Supreme Court of New Jersey
accepted for review the above two cases together
with a similar third case involving defendant
Strychnewicz.

In the Leonardis-Rose appeal to the Supreme
Court, they challenged the validity of the exclusionary criteria on equal protection grounds.
While the Court did not find it necessary to
make a determination on the equal protection arguments posed by the defendants, it did find the
criteria to be exclusionary. The Court stated:

We find that the exclusionary criteria
accord misplaced emphasis to the offense
with which a defendant is charged and
hence fail to emphasize the defendant's
potention for rehabilitation.[9]

The Court emphasized that the criteria really ignored such important factors as the defendant's willingness to avoid conviction and its
accompanying stigma by restricting their initial
consideration to an evaluation of the charges

brought against the defendants. The court went on to explain that:

> Because of these shortcoming and because we feel that the future utility of (pretrial diversion) is dependent upon its uniform implementation on a statewide basis, we reject the Bergen County exclusionary criteria as absolute standards by which to evaluate defendant's applications.[10]

Distinguishable from the issue raised by the Leonardis-Rose appeal, the companion Strychenewicz appeal presents the issue of whether a prosecutor may refuse to articulate his or her reasons for declining to consent to a defendant's admission into a pretrial diversion program.

Responding to the Strychenewicz issue, the New Jersey court held that prosecutors may not refuse to give reasons for their decisions and that "compelling a prosecutor to furnish reasons for his decision is not only consistent with the goals of (pretrial diversion), but tends to further their implementation."[11]

As a result of the findings in *Leonardis I*, the New Jersey court made the following modifications for implementation of diversion guidelines throughout the state:

> a. Defendants who have been accused of *any* crime shall be eligible for admission to a program.
> b. Defendant's admission to a (pretrial diversion) program should be measured according to his amenability to correction, responsiveness to rehabilitation and na-

ture of the offense with which he is charged.

c. Although a trial-type proceeding is not necessary, defendant shall be accorded an informal hearing before the designated judge for a county at every stage of a defendant's association with a (pretrial diversion) project at which his admission, rejection or continuation in the program is put in question. A disposition is appealable by leave of court as any interlocutory order. R. 2:2.[12]

In this opinion (*Leonardis I*), the court also suggested that a statement of reasons for diversion denial is imposed where administrative authorities seek to revoke privileges.[13] However, in a later case, *State v. Lebbing*,[14] the same New Jersey court was specifically faced with the issue of whether due process applies in pretrial diversion revocation situations. In its answer to this due process question, the court stated that in pretrial diversion termination hearings, minimal requirements of due process require that the procedural protections as spelled out by the United States Supreme Court in *Morrissey v. Brewer* and *Gagnon v. Scarpelli* are applicable.

It shall be inserted here that in the subsequent *Leonardis II*,[15] the court further stressed that in making any determination, the prosecutor's decisions in pretrial diversion matters are primarily individualistic in nature.

In 1979, the New Jersey Supreme Court decided *State v. Sutton*.[16] The defendant, the mother of two children aged 9 and 11, was charged with unlawfully receiving public assistance funds over a four and a half year period. The reason given by the prosecution for rejecting this applicant states that the offense for which she was charged is "....part of a continuing criminal business or enterprise."[17] The defendant contended that her crime did not constitute a "continuing business or enterprise" within the intended Guidelines of the New Jersey Supreme Court and emphasized her belief that others who had been charged with similar offenses had been granted admission into the pretrial diversion program.[18] The issue focused on in *Sutton* is whether the prosecutor's objection to the defendant's entry into the pretrial diversion program amounted to patent and gross abuse of prosecutorial discretion.

Relying on the standards established in *Leonardis I*, the *Sutton* court found that the "statement of reasons" provided to the defendant was deficient; and under the *Leonardis II* holding, the *Sutton* court found that neither the statement of reasons provided to the defendant nor the record of the hearing below shows that "individualistic" factors played any role in *the prosecutor's* decision.[19]

In summation, it seems clear - at least from this analysis of development of diversion cases in one state - that any pretrial diversion program involving court-related matters should be structured so that individual fundamental legal rights are not in jeopardy. For the most part, diversion programs have operated without very much legal challenge as to violations of constitutional rights. However, the growing emergence of court cases in this area dictate a need for more detailed legislative, judicial and administrative definitions of the rights of pretrial diversion participants.

[1] See Jonathan S. Feld, *Pretrial Diversion*: *Problems of Due Process and Weak Cases*, 59 Boston University, L.R. 305; Joseph B. Stulberg, *A Civil Alternative to Criminal Prosecution*, 52 Albany L.R. 359; Note, *Pretrial Diversion from the Criminal Process*, 83 Yale L.J. 827.

[2] *Id*.

[3] Rule 3.28 provided in relevant part: RULE 3.28 PRETRIAL INTERVENTION PROGRAMS
(a) In countries where a pretrial intervention program is approved by the Supreme Court for operation under this rule, the Assignment Judge shall designate a judge or judges to act on all matters pertaining to the program, with the exception, however, that the Assignment Judge shall him or herself act on all matters involving treason, murder, kidnapping, manslaughter, sodomy, rape, armed robbery, or sale or dispensing of narcotic drugs by persons not drug-dependent.
(b) Where a defendant charged with a penal or criminal offense has been accepted by the program, the designated judge may, on the recommendation of the Trial Court Administrator for the county, the Chief Probation Officer for the county, or such other person approved by the Supreme Court as program director, and with the consent of the prosecuting attorney and the defendant, postpone all further proceedings against said defendant on such charges for a period not to exceed 3 months. 363 A. 2d 321. Also see Yale L.J. 827 (1974) New Jersey.

[4] Stulberg.

[5] Id.

[6] 363 A. 321. (1976).

[7] The preface to, and first provision of the Bergen County PTI Project Exclusionary Criteria are as follows:

Flexible guidelines have been adopted which are designed to produce a class of participants most amenable to the precepts of this Project.

The focus of the Project is upon the possibilities of attitudinal and behavioral change of each defendant. Consequently, the Project will accept defendants charged with practically any offense. Some offenses, however are of sufficient severity to prejudice potential employers, incite society's vengeance or in some other manner render the defendant inappropriate for participation. Other offenses indicate a likelihood of psychological disorder. Persons who come within the following criteria must ordinarily be excluded:

A. *Type of Offense*:

1. Heinous Offenses: Atrocious Assault and Battery where the victim is seriously injured; Homicide; Mayhem; Forceable Rape; Assault and Battery on a Police Officer involving injury; Armed Robbery where the victim is injured; Sale of a Controlled Dangerous Substance. Although these offenses may not prejudice some employers, there is the additional factor of society's expectation in cases of this nature which may require exclusion. Id. at 324.

[8] Id. at 334-5.

[9] Id. at 335.

[10] Id.

[11] Id. at 336.

[12] Id. at 340.

[13] *Morrisey v. Brewer*, 408 U.S. 471, 92 S. Ct. 2593, 33 L.Ed. 2d 484 (1972) and *Gagnon v. Scarpelli*, 411 U.S. 778, 93 S. Ct. 1756, 36 L.Ed. 2d 656 (1973).

[*14*] 385 A. 2d 936 (1978).

[*15*] 375 A. 2d 607 (1977).

[*16*] 402 A. 2d 230.

[17] Id. at 232.

[18] Id. at 233.

[19] Such statements must meet the test of both facilitating judicial review of the prosecutorial determination and allowing a defendant a meaningful opportunity to rebut the premise upon which that determination is based.   363 A. 2d 321.

THE DILEMMA OF LEGAL VERSUS MORAL
RESPONSIBILITY AND THE INSANITY DEFENSE

> It is an old maxim that justice without
> understanding and mercy is cruelty, while
> understanding and mercy without justice
> corrode respect for law. Because of the
> limitations on our attempts to cope with
> mentally disordered offenders, we inevi-
> tably have neither justice nor under-
> standing, but end up with cruelty or with
> cynicism about the law - and often
> both.[1]

The insanity defense is undoubtedly the most
controversial and debated issue in Anglo-American jurisprudence. This chapter will attempt to
clarify and analyze the current status of the
insanity defense from an ethical and moral point
of view with a primary focus on the concepts of
legal and moral responsibility.

It is essential to realize that the notion
of responsibility is central to any discussion
of the insanity defense. Sagarin and Kelly
found that responsibility has been used synony-
mously for accountability. It is this sense of
accountability that is the concern of this chapter, for it is the presence or absence, or the
degree of accountability that morally justifies
punishment of the offender under our system of
law. Of concern relative to the insanity defense is whether or not there are conditions under which individuals should *not* be held accountable for their behavior. In order to

answer this question it is necessary to define as precisely as possible what responsibility is and then to differentiate between legal and moral responsibility.

Responsibility can be equated with praiseworthiness or blameworthiness of voluntary actions as Aristotle conceived it in his *Micomachean Ethics*. Aristotle excluded as either praiseworthy or blameworthy those acts which were involuntary, for whatever reason. Glover concluded that "An important feature of Aristotle's account of voluntary actions is that it includes acts occasioned by anger or desire: on this view we are not absolved from responsibility for an act because it is impulsive."[2] Furthermore, as Sagarin and Kelly note, "....Aristotle argued against a Calvinist conception of responsibility, a simple bipolar scheme, where one is either responsible or nonresponsible, where, in effect, individuals are mixtures of two dichotomous attributes, good and evil; rather, his accounts attempt to sketch those considerations and contingencies that are relevant factors in behavior and judging behavior."[3] Such an Airstotelian view of responsibility depicts responsibility as various shades of gray, rather than as black and white.

By contrast, our Anglo-American system of law, in the Calvinist tradition, has viewed responsibility as an all or nothing phenomenon. Our system, derived from Utilitarian philosophy, views the individual as a free agent exerting his will under conditions which make him accountable. Thus, under criminal law, if the individual is blameworthy for harms which come to others, he is punishable. The individual is punishable for the purpose of deterrence, which theoretically promotes the Utilitarian goal of the greatest happiness for the greatest number. Punishment, under this doctrine, is morally justifiable since the individual has acted on his own free will.[4] The goal of punishment is twofold: to render the individual more obedient to society's rules (specific of special deterrence) and to render others more obedient by indicating to them the consequences of such behavior (general deterrence).

The use of punishment for violations of the law from this view of responsibility assumes that the individual is a rational free being who wills or chooses the behaviors in which he engages. The questions which then arise are: Do all individuals, in fact, have the ability to rationally and freely exercise their wills to make choices? If not, under what conditions should individuals not be held accountable and punishable for their wrongs?

In order to answer these questions it is necessary to distinguish between the ideas of legal and moral responsibility. The Aristotelian conception of responsibility for this analysis is "moral responsibility." Consistent with this conception of moral responsibility, Hart stated, "....to say that a person is morally responsibile for something he has done or for some harmful outcome of his own or others' conduct, is to say that he is morally blameworthy, or morally obligated to make amends for the harm."[5] Hart defined legal responsibility by saying that for a man to be "....legally responsible for an act or harm is to state that his connection with the act or harm is sufficient according to law for liability."[6] Hart further stated that "....because a person is legally responsibile for some action he is liable to be punished for it."[7] It is important to realize that legal responsibility in a situation exists because a specific law exists, whereas moral responsibility exists separate from and transcends the existence of law.

Legal and moral responsibility are both present when a "true crime" is committed. A "true crime" is one in which there are both 1) the physical act or omission of an act in violation of a law, referred to as *actus reus* and 2) the mental element known as criminal intent, evil mind or *mens rea*. There are, as Gardner and Manian indicated, crimes which do not require the mental element such as those involving vehicular traffic, narcotics, liquor, sanitation, hunting, and purity of foods.[8] These are referred to as "strict liability" crimes, the conviction for which does not require intent be proven; the defendant is liable regardless of his or her state of mind at the time of the act.[9]

For those acts which are "true crimes", it is contended that the state is justified in punishing the individual because, as both *actus reus* and *mens rea* are present, the individual is considered both legally and morally responsibile. The legal responsibility or *actus reus* is empirically verifiable on the basis of testimony and evidence brought before the court. Moral responsibility, however, is dependent upon conditions not as easily empirically verifiable.

Of central concern here is the extent to which the individual had control over his conduct at the time the crime occurred. At this point, what Hart referred to as "capacity-responsibility" becomes an issue. Hart states:

"Because 'responsible for his actions' in this sense refers not to a legal status but to certain complex psychological characteristics of persons, a person's responsibility for his actions may intelligibly be said to be 'diminished' or 'impaired' as well as altogether absent and persons may be said to be 'suffering from diminished responsibility' much as a wounded man may be said to be suffering from a diminished capacity to control the movements of his limbs."[10] Thus, in any situation, for an individual to be held morally responsible for his actions he must possess substantial capacity-responsibility. It is believed that the absence of sufficient capacity-responsibility precludes moral responsibility, the requisite to justify punishing the individual for his illegal act.

It is because of the lack of capacity-responsibility that there are generally speaking two categories of individuals whom we do not hold criminally responsible. These are: children under the age of seven[11] and those who suffer from insanity, mental disease or defect. In the case of children, it is presumed that they possess neither the mental capacity to formulate criminal intent nor the ability to appreciate the wrongfulness of their actions. It is also assumed that the threat of formal punishment would not serve as a deterrent to children under the age of seven. Likewise, the insane or those suffering from severe mental disease or defect are presumed not to possess sufficient capacity-responsibility, as previously defined, to be held morally responsibile for their criminal acts and, like children, they are also considered undeterrable.

In those cases in which the sanity of the defendant has been a point of contention in the establishment of responsibility, a number of substantially different criteria have been utilized. In most situations where the traditional insanity criteria are used, defendants can be found not guilty by reason of insanity and thus absolved of responsibility if they did not know the difference between right and wrong or if they were unable to control their actions at the time of the crime. Some jurisdictions require the prosecution to prove sanity, while others require the defense to prove insanity, although there is a recent nationwide trend toward placing the burden of proof on the defendant.

State and federal jurisdictions rely on 19 variations of the four basic insanity defenses: the M'Naghten test, the irresistible impulse test, the Durham rule, and the substantial capacity test.

The M'Naghten test, popularly referred to as the right-wrong test, is the oldest and most restrictive of the insanity tests. The English House of Lords formulated the M'Naghten rule in 1843,[12] thereby setting a precedent in cases such as M'Naghten's in which the defense wishes absolution of criminal responsibility due to mental incapacity. The test of insanity states:

> (To) establish a defense on the ground of insanity, it must be clearly proved that, at the time of the committing of the act, the party accused was labouring under such a defect of reason, from disease of the mind, as not to know the nature and quality of the act he was doing; or, if did know it, that he did not know he was doing what was wrong.[13]

Under the M'Naghten test, culpability is based on the individual's rationality, i.e., the capacity to reason and the ability to distinguish between right and wrong. The M'Naghten criteria are consistent with Jonathan Edward's definition of a moral agent being one who possesses both a moral faculty (capability of distinguishing between right and wrong) and a capacity to reason.[14]

The irresistible impulse test, derived from an early Massachusetts case, is used as a supplement to the M'Naghten rule in some jurisdictions. This test of insanity states:

> If then it is proved, to the satisfaction of the jury, that the mind of the accused was in a diseased and unsound state, the question will be, whether the disease existed to so high a degree, that for the time being it overwhelmed the reason, conscience, and judgment, and whether the prisoner, in committing the criminal act, acted from an irresistible impulse; if so, then the act was not the act of a voluntary agent, but the involuntary act of the body, without the concurrence of the mind directing it.[15]

Under the irresistible impulse test, culpability is based on the individual's volition. This test addresses the issue of whether the defendant could have resisted the impulse even if there had been a police officer in uniform standing nearby and, thus, is often referred to as the policeman-at-the-elbow test.

Under this test, criminal responsibility is nullified if a mental disease prevented the defendant from controlling his behavior, even though the defendant knew the nature of the criminal act and was aware of its wrongfulness. The irresistible impulse, however, must have originated from a mental disease, not from an emotion, moral depravity, or criminal perversion.

In response to criticism by the psychiatric profession on the archaic model of the human psyche as a compartmentalized version of homunculi in the brain designating right and wrong, or control and impulse, a liberal federal judge, David Bazelon, supported a third version of the insanity defense in *Durham v. United States*.[16] The Durham rule recognized the modern conceptualization of the mind as an integrated whole; cognition and control. *Durham* held that a defendant was not criminally responsible if the unlawful act was the product of mental disease or mental defect and, thus, is known as the product test. Originally, under this test, the jury was instructed to reach a decision regarding two questions: whether the defendant was sane or insane at the time of the alleged offense and whether the offense was the "product" of the insanity.

Judge Bazelon maintained in *Durham* that the identification of specific symptoms was both irrelevant and futile and it was his intention to broaden psychiatric participation in the courtroom process. Predictably, psychiatrists reacted enthusiastically to this decision, while lawyers maintained that the Durham rule was so broad as to constitute practically a non-rule. The verbal battles which had surrounded the concepts of right and wrong in M'Naghten were optimistically expected to vanish.

This optimism was premature, however, as the Durham rule was not widely adopted in the United States. In 1956 Judge Bazelon ruled that rather than displacing the right-wrong test and the irresistible impulse test, the product test was merely supplementing them and, thus, the jury should be instructed as to the proper application of all three.[17]

By 1970, even Judge Bazelon questioned the efficacy of the Durham rule in *United States v. Brawner*.[18] This case clarified the previous ambiguity concerning the word "product" in *Durham* and the 1970 decision stated that there must be a relationship between the disease and the act, stressing that this relationship must be critical in a determinative or causal effect with regard to the act. Two years later, the same court which had first formulated the progressive *Durham* rule replaced this test with the Model Penal Code test in *United States v. Brawner*.[19]

The American Law Institute's Model Penal Code test, popularly referred to as the substantial capacity test, was formulated as a compromise between the existing tests of insanity. This test suggests a verdict of not guilty by reason of insanity if either the right-wrong or the irresistible impulse criterion is satisfied. Under the American Law Institute's draft, the defendant is released from responsibility under criminal law:

> ...at the time of such conduct as a result of mental disease or defect, he lacks substantial capacity either to appreciate the criminality wrongfulness of his conduct or to conform his conduct to the requirements of law.[20]

In addition to these four tests of insanity, the diminished responsibility test, although not an insanity test per se, is used in cases involving defendants with abnormal mental conditions not amounting to insanity as defined by the jurisdiction's statute. This test is used primarily in reducing charges from murder to manslaughter.[21]

Each new formulation of a legal test of insanity has paralleled the psychiatric state of knowledge regarding the human mind and, as Schur points out, our ever-increasing reverence for science and technology has resulted in an attempt to effect scientific justice.[22] As many critics acknowledge, however, modern psychiatry suggests that we are all a little "sick".[23] It is no longer obvious who is crazy and who is not and, as recognized in *McDonald v. United States*,[24] "....the term, mental disease or defect, has various meanings, depending upon how and why it is used, and by whom. Mental disease means one thing to a physician bent on treatment, but something different, if somewhat overlapping, to a court of law."

It is this "overlapping" between law and psychiatry, this merger of scientific expertise and the legal process, which culminates in our present dilemma of establishing responsibility when dealing with mentally disordered defendants. Illustrative of this is the fact that insanity is not included in the American Psychiatric Association's *Diagnostic and Statistical Manual of Mental Disorders*.[25] This is expected, however, as the concept of insanity is a legal term, not a psychiatric one.

Law and psychiatry, wedded in the adversarial milieu of the courtroom, are plagued by the

same formidable problem of many marriages - a
lack of communication. The disparate legacies
of free will and scientific determinism of the
Positive and Classical Schools of Criminology
which prompted Ferri to state succinctly, "we
speak two different languages,"[26] is represented in the insanity defense when law and psychiatry attempt to define insanity.

Each profession is esoteric, utilizing professional argot which precludes immediate com-
prehension by the other. Although evolving from
the same philosophical orientation in dealing
with deviant behavior, as Ross states,
"....lawyers and psychiatrists are incapable of
communication on some issues because the two
disciplines .... have taken the diverse paths of
pragmatic versus semantic, subjective versus objective, and prescriptive versus descriptive.
The logic, language, and orientation of each
discipline are in many ways incompatible.[27]

Psychiatrists, as scientists, are committed
to moral objectivity and neutrality, while one
of the primary functions of our criminal law is
the assessment of responsibility and guilt.
Blame, per se, is an irrelevant issue to the
psychiatrist, who typically seeks causative ex-
planations without regard to blaming the individual for the behavior.[28] Our legal system,
on the other hand, carries on the Classical
School tradition of the doctrine of free will.
This fundamental tenet of our system of justice
permeates every aspect of dealing with criminal
behavior, and as Roscoe Pound stated:

> Historically, our substantive criminal
> law is based on a theory of punishing the
> vicious will. It postulates a free agent

confronted with a choice between doing
right and doing wrong and choosing freely
to do wrong.[29]

In addition to the problems resulting from
the amalgam of law and psychiatry, there are
problems inherent in the insanity tests themselves. All four insanity tests cover two broad
components of human behavior: volition and cognition, with some tests emphasizing the voli-
tional capacity, (e.g., irresistible impulse)
and others emphasizing the cognitive faculty,
(e.g., M'Naghten). Irrespective of the differ-
ential emphasis, however, each has been accused
of having inadequacies.

The avalanche of criticism surrounding the
M'Naghten rule for the past 140 years has centered on its linguistics. There are obvious ambiguities regarding such concepts as "disease of
the mind" and "know" and these ambiguities have
allowed juries to adopt either a restrictive interpretation or a broad interpretation of the
rule, which results in inconsistent application
of the criteria. Appellate courts generally
adopt a broad interpretation of "know"[30] and,
as Morris noted, if "know" is broadly interpreted to include both intellectual and affective
knowledge, in accordance with our present conceptualization of an integrated personality,
then one primary criticism of M'Naghten's re-
strictiveness is countered.[31]

Likewise, although emphasizing the volition-
al component of behavior and although considered
by some people to be an improvement over M'-
Naghten, the irresistible impulse test has been
criticized for failing to adequately extend M'-
Naghten. Morris maintains that the lack of vol-

ition mandated by the irresistible impulse test equates the act with a muscular spasm for which an individual is rightly held blameless[32] but this analogy, according to Fingarette, is an invalid one, as "....a mere physical force is purposeless, nonintelligent. Such a force may have direction, but this is purely spatial direction; it is not the 'psychological' kind of direction that we call 'purpose' or 'intent' or 'meaning'.[33] In addition to this criticism, the irresistible impulse test has also been criticized for the connotation of "impulse", which implies sudden onset, thereby being inapplicable to behavior which results from the long-term brooding of a mentally ill defendant.[34]

The Durham rule has been criticized for its broadness, as this test presents no definitive standard by which a jury can weigh the evidence regarding the defendant's mental state.[35] Furthermore, Durham's "product" has been accused of suffering from the same ambiguity as M'Naghten's criteria.

Although the Model Penal Code test rejects the Durham rule because of its ambiguous "product", many critics maintain that the "result" of the substantial capacity test of the Model Penal Code is reminescent of Durham's "product" insofar as ambiguity is concerned.[36] Furthermore, interchanging "criminality" with "wrongfulness" presents an ever greater problem.

It should be remembered that wrongfulness may be defined legally by criminal statute, morally by the harm principle as formulated by Mill in 1859, and subjectively by the non-rational individual functioning under a delusion. Criminality is defined by the legal code, while wrongfulness is defined by the moral code. In our system there is no perfect correlation between what is wrong and what is criminal and although it is legitimately contended there is a difference between wrongfulness and criminality (an act may be criminal but not necessarily wrong), in most cases involving the insanity defense, the crimes are of a sufficiently serious nature as to make "society's moral judgment identical with the legal standard."[37] This distinction, however, does nothing to resolve the issue of whether the defendant's responsibility for the act should be determined by his ability to understand that the act is legally wrong or morally wrong.

Many mentally disordered defendants may be fully cognizant of the law's prescription, yet believe their actions were morally justified due to their delusions resulting from their mental diseases or defects. Morris concluded that, "There are very few people who don't appreciate that it is against the law to shoot somebody. If you ask all the inhabitants of mental hospitals who can speak whether killing a person is wrong, they would say, 'Of course it is'."[38]

This is consistent with the argument that a person may possess intellectual knowledge of right and wrong and still be incapable of understanding the social significance of right and wrong. Goldstein maintains that knowing the "quality of an act, with all its social and emotional implication, requires more than an abstract, purely intellectual knowledge."[39] This contention has also been supported by Cleckley, particularly when dealing with the psychopathic defendant, who may be quite adept at assuming a mask of sanity, yet quite incapable of any practical moral application of the rules of conduct he so adroitly espouses. This is what Johns and Quay refer to as: "knowing the words but not the music."[40]

Beginning with M'Naghten, the courts have traditionally relied on expert psychiatric testimony in order to clarify whether mentally disordered defendants did, in fact, "know" right from wrong or whether they could have controlled their behavior. Many people, however, have become increasingly critical of the role of psychiatrists as expert witnesses. These critics allege that psychiatric expert testimony is a misnomer, as psychiatric testimony is more akin to swearing contests between psychiatrists for the defense and psychiatrists for the prosecution, each arriving at opposite conclusions regarding the defendant's state of mind at the time of the offense.[41] Szasz, a psychiatrist, acrimoniously describes psychiatrists in the courtroom as "hired guns" and "fakes."[42] These opponents of psychiatric testimony maintain that psychiatric testimony is inadequate in sufficiently clarifying the issue of whether a mentally disordered defendant should be held responsible for his behavior.

Even Judge Bazelon, who played the devil's advocate in broadening the role of psychiatry in the courtroom has become disenchanted. Issuing an apologia, Judge Bazelon criticized psychiatry's continued reliance on incomprehensible terminology, its insistence on labeling behavior, and its preoccupation with vague probabilities in lieu of concrete facts. Although Judge Bazelon adamantly supported psychiatry as a science twenty years before, he has accused it of being a mystical art, inherently plagued by uncertainty.

Just as Judge Bazelon has become disenchanted with psychiatry, many have become disenchanted with the insanity defense and, as a result of John Hinckley's successful use of the defense, emotional cries for abolition of the defense have been exacerbated.[43] Before we succumb to emotionalism, however, we must rationally examine two questions from a moral perspective.

First, should the insanity defense be abolished? Second, if the insanity defense is not to be abolished, should it, in some way, be modified so as to result in better protection for the public, such that violent offenders acquitted on the basis of insanity be subjected to long-term treatment? This would help to insure that such individuals would not present a further threat to the public.

An answer to this first question regarding the abolition of the insanity defense has been insightfully presented by Fingarette:

> As I see it, the fundamental reason for resisting the move to abolish these defenses is that they reflect the very soul of our legal system. The insanity plea is the litmus test of our commitment to the idea of citizen responsibility under law. To hold an insane or mentally disabled person responsible to the law in the same way we hold citizens to it generally is to make a mockery of the idea of responsibility.[44]

The abolition of the insanity defense would represent a move to effectively ignore *mens rea*, the moral component of law and criminal responsibility. This would, as Fingarette suggests, reduce law to "merely a device for social control."[45] All crimes would, thus, be "strict liability" acts for which criminal intent would be irrelevant.

There is another dilemma which surfaces if the insanity defense is abolished. Without the insanity defense, which provides an alternative verdict for judges or juries, there would only be two alternatives: find the individual innocent of convict an individual whose moral responsibility is highly questionable. It is quite likely that such a situation would result in: 1) more "hung juries," thus greater cost to the state for retrials; 2) a greater tendency for judges and juries (where permissible) to convict the defendant on a lesser charge in an attempt to reduce punishment because they perceive a partial mitigation of moral responsibility due to mental defect and; 3) either the injustices of punishment of the non-responsible or total vindication and freedom for those who deserve some form of punishment or who, for the sake of societal protection, should be in some way incapacitated.

Were the insanity defense abolished and *mens rea* not an element to be proven, it is conceivable that the next step could be to ignore all mitigating circumstances and simply treat all criminal acts of a certain type uniformly. Under such conditions, if *actus reus* were proven, everyone found guilty of the same crime would receive the same punishment. This would be what the early Utilitarians envisioned as "equal punishments for equal crimes." However, given the current state of our knowledge that human behavior is differentially caused or influenced by innumerable factors, this alternative is morally untenable. Thus, if abolition of the insanity defense is not an acceptable alternative, what is?

One response to the outcry to abolish the insanity defense is the plea or verdict, "guilty but mentally ill." A defendant could then plead "guilty but mentally ill" and if this plea is accepted, he can be treated in either of two ways. First, he could be committed to the custody of the state department of corrections, where he would undergo thorough diagnosis, be treated, and upon completion of successful treatment be made to serve out the remainder of his sentence as any other prisoner, or, second, he could be remanded to the state department of mental health for treatment and upon completion of successful treatment he would be transferred back to the custody of the department of corrections to serve the remainder of his sentence in a correctional facility. The individual can also be found "guilty but mentally ill" if he originally entered a plea of "not guilty by reason of insanity", such as in the state of Michigan, the first state to enact a "guilty but mentally ill" statute. This statute says:

> If a defendant asserts a defense of insanity ... the defendant may be found "guilty but mentally ill" if, after trial, the trier of fact finds all of the following beyond a reasonable doubt:
>
> a. That the defendant is guilty of an offense
> b. That the defendant was mentally ill at the time of the commission of that offense

c. That the defendant was not legally insane at the time of the commission of the offense.[46]

For statutory purposes, mental illness is defined as "a substantial disorder of thought or mood which significantly impairs judgment, behavior, capacity to recognize reality, or abilty to cope with the demands of life."

If the individual who originally plead "not guilty by reason of insanity" is found "guilty but mentally ill", the judge or jury is, in effect, saying he did possess the "substantial capacity either to appreciate the criminality (wrongfulness) of his conduct or to conform his conduct to the requirements of law" (Model Penal Code criteria.) Thus, the disorder of thought or mood was apparently not sufficient in the minds of the judge or jury to cause the defendant to be incapable of forming the *mens rea* necessary to hold him morally responsible. Stated differently, the individual apparently still possesses sufficient "capacity-responsibility", as defined by Hart such that though his responsibility was "diminished" or "impaired", the individual could still differentiate right from wrong to the extent that he should, after sufficient treatment, be punished for his wrongdoing.

There are those who say, as does Slowinski, that the "guilty but mentally ill" verdict has not eliminated the traditional insanity defense, that defendants can still be found legally insane at the time of the offense and be relieved of all criminal responsibility. There are, however, two real possibilities for injustices relative to "truly insane" defendants. First, as Slowinski points out, "jurors, who often view the insanity defense with suspicion, will ignore evidence on the absence of *mens rea* in some cases and return a verdict which they believe will provide needed treatment for a person who has asserted his own insanity, while providing protection to society from a person who has committed a criminal act."[47] Secondly, Slowinski suggests that jurors may not be able to draw a distinction between "mental illness" and "insanity" and, thus, mistakenly find insane defendants "guilty but mentally ill."[48] If as Slowinski suggests, "the insanity defense is a constitutional right, such abuse and confusion would deprive some defendants of that right."[49]

In addition to these potential injustices, it should be noted that the "guilty but mentally ill" verdict may result in a violation of the cruel and unusual punishment provision of the Eighth Amendment for those who were not capable of understanding the wrongfulness of their criminal action. Further, as Slowinski points out, defendants "who are sentenced to prison under the guilty but mentally ill provision will not receive adequate treatment for their continuing insanity, since treatment at prisons is less comprehensive and beneficial than treatment at mental institutions."[50] In addition, if those who are "mentally ill" also meet the criteria of being unable to appreciate the wrongfulness of their actions, then those individuals will be criminally punished for acts where there was no criminal intent.

In retrospect, the "guilty but mentally ill" verdict seems to be political rhetoric, with great potentialities for immoral and unjust outcomes. If the manifest purpose is incapacitation of "dangerous offenders", it would seem that this goal could be obtained without any pretense of concern for treatment which ultimately results in punishment. The "guilty but mentally ill" alternative seems to be a form of moral fraud since it results in punishment of those who should not be held morally responsible for their acts.

The rebuttal to this accusation can and will be that since psychiatry lacks the precision to assess the extent to which individuals' self-control may or may not be impaired as the result of a "mental illness or defect", what difference does it make? This, too, is a cop-out because we know that there are and have been numerous cases of individuals whose behavior would be termed insane by any of all of the insanity tests yet devised. Since we have morally justified the existence of an insanity defense, by the same criteria, we can define the notion of "guilty but mentally ill" as unacceptable.

The remaining question regarding the present status of the insanity defense is, are there any morally and practically viable alternatives? The answer is relatively simple and is based on numerous points which have been discussed previously. First, since psychiatric knowledge can be characterized as vague and imprecise, it seems that the role of psychiatry in the determination of criminal responsibility should be diminished, at least with respect to determining whether the individual could, in the words of the Model Penal Code criteria, "conform his conduct to the requirements of law." Psychiatry is, as Bartol noted, ".... in no position to determine the degree of personal control demonstrated during some past incident. Therefore, we cannot determine whether an individual involved in a crime was functioning under free will or 'lack of control' in any particular situation.[51]

Furthermore, there seems to be no way to determine who are the undeterred and who are the undeterrable or who could have resisted impulses and who could not, or who possessed substantially diminished capacity and who did not. Thus, the question of the individual's ability to control his behavior should be eliminated from consideration in the insanity defense, thus leaving as the sole element of contention, *mens rea* or appreciation of the wrongfulness of the act, for the determination of moral and criminal responsibility. Bonnie concluded that this is the "necessary and sufficient test of criminal responsibility."[52] It is, after all, an assumption of our legal system that normal adults understand and are appreciative of the moral and legal rightness or wrongness of their actions. Since the defendant, by entering a plea of not guilty by reason of insanity is admitting factual guilt, it seems that in order to be absolved of moral guilt or responsibility the individual should bear the burden of proof of his abnormal condition.

Although individuals should not be punished for acts for which they are not responsible, it is morally incumbent upon society to make every attempt to protect its citizens from individuals who, by their past behavior, may represent a real danger. For those individuals whose potential for harmful behavior is high, total incapacitation is mandatory. For those individuals who seem to respond positively to treatment, the amount of supervision and incapacitation should be gradually diminished as it is believed the individual is becoming more trustworthy and morally blameworthy for his actions. It is mandatory that if an error is to occur regarding treatment of those diagnosed insane, that the error is to be in the direction of more rather than less incapacitation and supervision.

The proposed modification of the insanity defense results in criteria which allow for a determination of criminal responsibility which are much the same as the M'Naghten rule. It is, however, suggested that total incapacity to appreciate the wrongfulness of the act should not be required. The incapacity must be judged, however, to be sufficiently substantial to negate moral responsibility. Also, by eliminating the concern for the individual's ability to voluntarily control his behavior, it is hoped that psychiatric testimony will be limited to statements of fact, rather than broad conclusory pronouncements which ar e based on unqualified supposition regarding the ability to control one's behavior.

Finally, although the phrase "substantial capacity to appreciate the wrongfulness of his act" is vague and lacks clarity and precision, so, unfortunately, is the present state of our knowledge about human behavior. Vagueness and ambiguity may be necessary components of any insanity test until reliable and valid empirical tests of responsibility can be devised but, as Allen notes, we may have a long wait, as:

> behavioral sciences have not advanced far enough to provide answers to such questions as moral culpability, dangerousness and treatability. But if we are awaiting

a scientific breakthrough on questions of moral blameworthiness, we will doubless still be waiting on Judgment Day (when, presumably, the only authoritative decision on that score will be issued.)[53]

Until that day, in the interest of justice, what is of paramount importance is that an insanity defense be maintained and that, as a civilized society, we do everything possible to avoid punishing those who are not morally responsible for their actions.

[1] Gambino, Richard. The murderous mind: In-
    sanity vs. the law. In Donald E.J. MacNama-
    ra (ed.) *Criminal Justice 80/81*. Guilford,
    Ct.: Dushkin Publishing Group, Inc., 1980,
    p. 149.

[2] Glover, Jonathan. *Responsibility*. London:
    Routledge and Degan Paul, 1970, p. 5.

[3] Sagarin, Edward and Kelly, Robert J. Moral
    responsibility and the law: An existential
    account. In H. Lawrence Ross (ed.) *Law
    and Deviance*. Beverly Hills, Ca.: Sage
    Publis., 1981, p. 24.

[4] The retributivist would say that this is the
    punishment the individual deserved in the
    sense of distributive justice (to each what
    is due him).

[5] Hart, H.L.A. *Punishment and Responsibili-
    ty: Essays in the Philosophy of Law*. New
    York: Oxford University Press, 1968, p. 225.

[6] Ibid., p. 222.

[7] Ibid.

[8] Gardner, Thomas J. and Manian. *Criminal
    Law: Principles, Cases and Readings*. St.
    Paul, Mn: West Publishing Company, 1980, p.
    42.

[9] The fact that the individual can be punished
    for the commission of "strict liability" of-
    fenses (where intent is not relevant) seems
    morally questionable, but this issue goes
    beyond the scope of the present chapter.

[10] Hart, H.L.A., p. 228.

[11] Some states have raised the age of criminal culpability to nine, ten and even twelve years of age.

[12] For a description of this case, see: Morris, Grant H. *The Insanity Defense: A Blueprint for Legislative Reform*. Lexington, Mass: D.C. Heath and Co., 1975.

[13] 10 Clark & Fin. 200, 8 Eng. Rep. 717 (1843).

[14] Schafer, Stephan. The problem of free will in criminology. *The Journal of Criminal Law and Criminology*. 1976, 67, No. 1, p. 484.

[15] Boyce, Ronald & Perkins, Rollin M. *Criminal Law and Procedure*. Mineola: Foundation Press, 1977, p. 552.

[*16*] 214 F. 2d 862, 871 (1954).

[17] 239 F. 2d 52 D.C. Cir. (1956).

[*18*] 436 F. 2d 200 (1970).

[*19*] 471 F. 2d 969 (1972).

[20] Although the current ALI standard states: ....lacked substantial capacity either to appreciate the wrongfulness of that conduct or to conform that conduct to the requirements of the law., many jurisdictions continue to use the 1962 proposed draft, wherein wrongfulness and criminality are

interchanged.

[21] Morris, Grant H., *The Insanity Defense: A Blueprint for Legislative Reform*. Lexington, Ma: D.C. Heath & Co., 1975.

[22] Schur, Edwin M. *Law and Society*. New York: Random House, 1968.

[23] Bartol, Curt R. *Criminal Behavior: A Psychosocial Approach*. Englewood Cliffs, N.J.: Prentice-Hall, 1980, and Szasz, Thomas. The myth of mental illness. *American Psychologist*, 1960, 15, 113-118.

[24] 114 U.S. App. D.C. 120, 312 F. 2d. 847, 851 (en banc, 1962).

[25] American Psychiatric Association. *Diagnostic and Statistical Manual of Mental Disorders*. Third Edition, Washington, D.C.: APA, 1980.

[26] Ferri, Enrico. *The Positive School of Criminology*. Chicago, Il.: Charles M. Keer and Co., 1913, p. 35.

[27] Ibid., p. 1.

[28] Menninger, Karl. *The Crime of Punishment*. New York: Viking Press, 1966.

[29] Pound, Roscoe. *Criminal Justice in Cleveland*. Cleveland, Oh.: The Cleveland Foundation, 1922, p. 586.

[30] Goldstein, Abraham S. *The Insanity Defense*. New Haven: Yale University Press,

1967.

[31] Morris, G.

[32] Morris, Arval. Criminal insanity. *Washington Law Review*, 1967, 43, p. 612.

[33] Fingarette, Herbert. *The Meaning of Criminal Insanity*. Berkeley, Ca: University of California Press, p. 161.

[34] Morris, G.

[35] Goldstein, A.

[36] Morris, G.

[37] Goldstein, A., p. 52.

[38] Morris, Norval. Abolish the insanity defense? *U.S. News & World Report*. 1982, p. 15.

[39] Goldstein, A.

[40] Johns, J.H. & Quay, H.C. The effect of social reward on verbal conditioning in psychopatic military offenders. *Journal of Consulting Psychology*, 1962, 26, p. 218.

[41] Shur, E., and Gambino, R.

[42] Szasz, Thomas. How Dan White got away with murder. In Donal E.J. MacNamara (ed.), *Criminal Justice 80/81*. Guilford, Ct.: Duskin Publishing Group, Inc., 1980, p. 161-162.

[43] Butler, Edward F. Insanity as a defense: after Hinckley. *The Tennessee Trial Lawyer*, in press August, 1983.

[44] Fingarette, Herbert. *The Meaning of Criminal Insanity*. p. 229-230.

[45] Ibid., p. 230.

[46] Michigan Comp. Laws 768.36(1) (Mich. Stat. Ann. 28.1059(1))

[47] Slowinski, Kenneth. Criminal responsibility: Changes in the insanity defense and the 'guilty but mentally ill' response. *Washburn Law Journal*, 1982, 21, p. 550.

[48] This is a distinct possibility, as even psychiatrists find it difficult to reach an agreement on a diagnosis.

[49] Slowinski, K., p. 550-551.

[50] Ibid., p. 551.

[51] Bartol, C., p. 174-175.

[52] Bonnie, Richard J. The moral basis of the insanity defense. *American Bar Association Journal*. 1983 February, 69, p. 197.

[53] Allen, Richard C. Abolition of the insanity defense. In Richard C. Allen, Elyce Zenoff Ferster & Jesse G. Rubin (eds.) *Readings in Law and Psychiatry*. Baltimore: Johns Hopkins Univ. Press, p. 708.

PLEA-BARGAINING:
CONTRADICTION OR JUSTICE?

The advent of the plea bargaining process has transformed the traditional model of criminal justice from an impartial trier of fact, which determined guilt or innocence after a formal adversarial trial,[1] to a process in which guilt is an agreement reached through informal negotiations between the prosecutor and defense counsel.[2] Subsequently, the quality of justice has been relegated to the plea negotiation process and determined by who formulated and on what basis the bargaining decision was developed.

Plea bargaining involves an agreement between the prosecutor and defense counsel[3] in which the defendant pleads guilty in return for a concession or concessions from the prosecutor.[4] The process, however is not new.[5] In fact, it has always been present in the criminal law process.[6]

The plea bargaining concession offered by the prosecutor may involve one or more of: 1) a recommendation for a reduced sentence, 2) a dismissal of additional charges, 3) an acceptance of a plea to a lesser included offense, or 4) the recommendation of a specific sentence acceptable to the defendant.[7] In return the defendant pleads guilty or no contest to the charge. In general, all plea bargaining involves leniency for the offender in return for a plea of guilty.[8] Also, while plea bargaining has been considered wholesale justice it has simultaneously become the very essence of the American criminal justice system.[9]

Initially, plea bargaining is informal and the participants are reluctant to comment upon their discussion. Their reluctance to discuss plea bargaining negotiations has created a low visibility process.[10] The result has been that the exact number of criminal cases settled through plea bargaining is unknown. The United States Courts Annual Report[11] estimated that in the federal district courts, from July 1972 through June 1973, 75 per cent of the criminal cases were disposed of by guilty pleas. Estimates for urban areas have been that 85 per cent of all criminal and 90 to 95 per cent of all felony cases, in which guilty pleas were entered, involved some for of plea negotiation.[12] Although plea bargaining practices[13] vary between jurisdictions,[14] conviction by guilty plea is normal and the criminal trial is the exception.[15] Society's inattention to post-arrest processes has reinforced the erroneous assumption that formal judicial proceedings (criminal trials) automatically followed an arrest.[16]

Prosecutorial Discretion

The prosecutors have been the most important individuals in the plea bargaining process.[17] They determine which cases to bargain and what concessions to offer or accept. One of the primary criticisms of plea bargaining has been its low visibility decision making process[18] and what information is used by prosecutors for their decisions.[19]

The primary consideration in whether or not to plea bargain should be the relative strength of the evidence against the defendant.[20]

However, the factors considered are: 1) reliability and admissibility of evidence,[21] 2) the defendant's prior criminal record,[22] and 3) the propriety of the police activity surrounding the case.[23]

Prosecutors have been more inclined to plea bargain cases which they may lose than cases which they can win.[24] Also, prosecutors do not formulate bargaining decisions exactly alike. What may appear to be a weak case to one may be a stronger case to another. In addition, prosecutors will not act the same in all cases.[25] A major concern in the plea bargaining process is that the decisions vary between assistant prosecutors working in the same office. For the most part no standards or guidelines exist and plea bargaining decisions are solely a matter of the individual prosecutor's discretion.[26]

The disparity between prosecutor's discretionary judgments are highly visible when a defendant charged with a minor offense encounters an obstinate prosecutor and receives as severe a disposition as a defendant charged with a serious offense whose case is handled by a lenient prosecutor. Discretionary disparity between prosecutors has also caused trial delays as defense counsels wait to determine if they may encounter a more lenient prosecutor in the future.

The nature and intent of the criminal process permits discretion on the part of the individual prosecutor.[27] In addition, aggravating factors which were designed to limit bargaining include the severity of the crime and seriousness of the victim's injury.[28] Clearly these are relative terms which could be interpreted differently by different prosecutors. What to one may seem a severe crime may not seem severe to another and in such a case the bargaining practices of the two will be different. Subsequently, plea bargaining discretion is more a refined *subjective adjustment* to a particular crime and offender than the *objective application* of the rules of law.[29]

Plea Bargaining Inducements

Generally, the defendants' bargaining positions are weak and the only benefit they can confer to the criminal justice system by pleading guilty is saving the prosecution time, expense of a trial, and foreclosing any risk of acquittal. The primary inducements for defendants to plead guilty are charge reductions or dismissals[30] and favorable sentence recommendations.[31] Additional plea bargaining inducements include the prosecutor's agreement: 1) not to prosecute the defendant's accomplices, 2) to a stipulation that the defendant serve in the armed forces, 3) not to oppose probation or a suspended sentence, 4) to recommend that the defendant serve his sentence in a particular rehabilitation program, or 5) that the defendant be adjudicated in a juvenile court.

In exchange for the guilty plea the defendant may agree to: 1) forego appeal, 2) cooperate with the police, 3) supply additional information to the prosecutor, or 4) testify as a witness in a subsequent trial. The defendants benefit in plea negotiations by: 1) avoiding extended pretrial incarceration anxieties and uncertainties of trial, 2) securing a speedy case disposition and the opportunity to acknowledge their guilt, and 3) a prompt beginning toward realizing whatever potential there may be for rehabilitation. The criminal justice system benefits as judges and prosecutors conserve vital resources. Also, the public is reasonably protected from potential risks posed by offenders charged with criminal offenses, but who remain at large, on bail, while awaiting completion of criminal proceedings.[32]

Judicial Discretion

Normally, the court will accede to the recommendations of the prosecutor and a judge will rarely reject a bargained guilty plea.[33] In fact, the decision in *United States v. Ammidown* severly limits the reasons a federal court judge may cite to reject a bargained plea.[34] Therefore, although judges are required to ratify any plea bargain they are limited in their latitude to reject negotiated pleas. For all practical purposes the bargaining decisions rest with the prosecutors and defense counsels. The judicial involvement operates only as a minimal control over the prosecutor.[35]

Sentencing Disparity

The defendants pleading guilty often receive a lesser sentence than they would have received had they exercised their constitutional right to a trial and been convicted.[36] The resulting sentencing differentials have an inhibiting effect on the exercise of the defendant's constitutional rights.[37]

However, sentencing differentials have been justified on the belief that an acknowledgement of guilt by a defendant is his first step toward rehabilitation.[38] Also, there is an indication that defendants commit varying degrees of perjury during trial testimony.[39] Subsequently, sentencing differentials are potential deterrents to frivolous defenses in the face of overwhelming evidence of guilt.[40] More importantly, the opportunity for a reduced sentence is the defendant's main inducement for plea bargaining. The overriding interests of defendants who plead guilty is to minimize their punishment[41] and the majority are successful.[42] However, Jacob,[43] advocated that bench or jury trials and subsequent convictions awarded comparable sentences as were plea bargained in similar offenses.

The Constitutionality of Plea Bargaining

In *Blackledge v. Allison*[44] and *Santobello v. New York*[45] the United States Supreme Court suggested that plea negotiations were an essential component of the administration of justice and under appropriate safeguards did not abridge the constitutional rights of the defendant. However, it is only recently that negotiated pleas have received attention from courts and approval of state legislatures.[46] The United States Supreme Court implied its approval of the plea bargaining process in *Brady v. United States*[47] by declining to invalidate Brady's conviction solely because it was the result of a plea bargain. In *Santobello v. New York* the Court clearly expressed its approval of the plea bargaining process. Furthermore, the Court concluded that a guilty plea induced by improper promises (*Brady v. United States*), threats (*Wally v. Johnson*),[48] or physical or mental coercion (*Von Moltke v. Gillies*)[49] which deprived it of the character of a voluntary act, would be void (*Machibroda v. United States*).[50]

Thus, the United States Supreme Court has upheld the constitutionality of the plea bargaining process, even though there are indications that the concept of plea bargaining violates the fundamental legal principle that a confession extracted in exchange for a promise of charge or sentence reduction is inadmissible. Nevertheless, this principle has not been applied in determining the voluntariness of the negotiated guilty plea. The accepted guilty plea, similar to the most incriminating confession, convicts the accused.[51]

The 1975 amended Federal Rules of Criminal Procedure included plea bargaining guidelines and indicated that the attorneys for the government and the defendant may engage in discussions with a view toward reaching an agreement that, upon the entering of a plea of guilty or no contest to a lesser charged offense or to a related offense, the attorney for the government may: 1) move for dismissal of other charges, 2) make a recommendation or agree not to oppose the defendant's request for a particular sentence, or 3) agree that a specific sentence is the appropriate case disposition.[52] The parties are required to disclose the terms of the agreement in open court, at which time the court may either accept or reject the agreement. If the court rejects the agreement, the defendant may withdraw the plea and request a full trial or may persist in the plea with the understanding that the court is not bound by the terms of the agreement.[53]

The Problem

The primary concern with plea bargaining has not been that some offenders received lesser sentences than may have been given after trial and conviction, but that, due to a lack of formal guidelines, there is no consistency in plea negotiation agreements between prosecutors within the same jurisdiction, between jurisdictions within the same state, or between states. Justice, then, is determined more by geographical location and fate than by the offender's action against society.

The State Attorney Generals or corresponding offices from 50 states and Puerto Rico contributed their rules of criminal procedure or statutes involving plea negotiations. These procedures and statutes were analyzed to assess plea negotiation inclusion in state law, case law, rules of criminal procedure, and uniformity between states.

Plea negotiations are authorized by statute in 1 state (2 per cent, Oregon) and prohibited in 1 state (2 per cent, Alaska). The remaining 48 states and Puerto Rico do not directly refer to plea negotiations in their statutes. However, 6 states (12 per cent) encourage the use of plea negotiations through case law while 1 state (2 per cent, Alabama) discourages them.

Approximately half the states (46 per cent) and Puerto Rico are guided by rules of criminal

TABLE 1 - PLEA BARGAINING

	Authorized or Prohibited by Statute	Discouraged or Encouraged by Case Law	Guided by rules of Criminal Procedure	Appeals Permitted from Guilty Plea
Alabama		Discouraged		
Alaska	Prohibited			
Arizona			Yes	
California		Encouraged		
Colorado			Yes	
Connecticut			Yes	
Delaware		Encouraged		
Florida			Yes	
Georgia				
Hawaii			Yes	
Idaho		Encouraged		
Illinois			Yes	
Indiana			Yes	
Iowa			Yes	
Kansas				
Kentucky			Yes	
Louisiana			Yes	
Maine			Yes	
Maryland			Yes	
Massachussetts				
Michigan				
Minnesota		Encouraged		
Mississippi				
Missouri			Yes	
Montana		pending		
Nebraska				
Nevada				
New Hampshire				
New Jersey		Encouraged	Yes	Yes
New Mexico			Yes	
New York				
North Carolina				Yes
North Dakota			Yes	
Ohio				
Oklahoma				
Oregon	Authorized			
Pennsylvania			Yes	
Rhode Island				
South Carolina				
South Dakota			Yes	
Tennessee				
Texas			Yes	
Utah				
Vermont				
Virginia			Yes	
Washington				
West Virginia				
Wisconsin		Encouraged		
Wyoming			Yes	
Puerto Rico			Yes	

TABLE 1 - PLEA BARGAINING (continued)

Provisions included for:

	Content Control	Disclosure in Court	Withdrawal of Plea	Voluntariness Test
Alabama				
Alaska				
Arizona				
Arkansas		Yes	Yes	Yes
California				
Connecticut	Yes	Yes		Yes
Delaware				
Florida	Yes	Yes	Yes	Yes
Georgia				
Hawaii	Yes		Yes	Yes
Idaho				
Illinois		Yes	Yes	Yes
Indiana	Yes			
Iowa		Yes		Yes
Kansas				
Kentucky			Yes	Yes
Louisiana				
Maine	Yes	Yes	Yes	Yes
Maryland	Yes	Yes	Yes	Yes
Massachussetts				
Michigan				
Minnesota				
Mississippi				
Missouri	Yes	Yes	Yes	Yes
Montana				
Nebraska				
Nevada				
New Hampshire				
New Jersey	Yes	Yes	Yes	
New Mexico	Yes	Yes	Yes	Yes
New York				
North Carolina			Yes	
North Dakota		Yes	Yes	Yes
Ohio				
Oklahoma				
Oregon	Yes		Yes	
Pennsylvania		Yes	Yes	Yes
Rhode Island				
South Carolina				
South Dakota	Yes	Yes	Yes	
Tennessee				
Texas		Yes		
Utah				
Vermont				
Virginia	Yes	Yes	Yes	Yes
Washington				
Wisconsin				
Wyoming	Yes	Yes	Yes	Yes
Puerto Rico				

procedure. The rules of criminal procedure permit appeals from guilty pleas in 2 states (4 per cent), control the content of plea negotiations in 13 states (26 per cent), require disclosure of plea agreements in open court in 16 states (32 per cent), allow withdrawal of the negotiated guilty plea in 17 states (34 per cent), and in 15 states (30 per cent) require an assessment of the negotiated guilty plea's voluntariness.

While the plea bargaining process has, to a large extent, come to the public's attention in the last decade, the decisions remain formulated in secret. Only the final agreement is presented in open court. The discussions and methods used to reach those agreements remain unknown. The majority of the process lies within the realm of prosecutorial discretion, which has been a vague and uncertain area of inquiry. Also, prosecutors have been reluctant to disclose how or why they make specific bargaining decisions.

In contrast to the support of the plea bargaining concept, there has been significant resistance to its practice. The overriding argument in opposition to plea bargaining is that the process limits the presumption of innocence.[54] This can be supported by tracing the actions of the prosecutor. The prosecutors propose plea negotiations on the assumption that the defendant is guilty. By operating in this manner the prosecution conflicts with the American legal premise of being innocent until proven guilty.

Plea bargaining is primarily an administrative activity rather than an adversarial confrontation and not open to public review. Subsequently, there is a high risk of abuse resulting from negotiations consumated in private.[55] The overcharging practices and threats of maximum sentence recommendations, for example, reduce the validity of plea bargaining. The concern regarding coercion during plea negotiations is legitimate and the fear is reinforced by the realization that the prosecution aggressively attempts to produce a favorable conviction rate.

The United States Supreme Court has recognized that the plea bargaining procedure is replete with potential abuses and has attempted to protect the defendant's constitutional rights.[56] In *Kercheval v. United States*,[57] the Court explicitly required federal and state judges to record the voluntary and intelligent waiver of the right to a jury trial, self incrimination, and the right to confront one's ac-cusers, before accepting guilty pleas. However in the majority of states (96 per cent) there is no constitutional or statutory right to appeal from a plea-based conviction; and in other states the right to appeal is limited.[58] The process of appeal in plea bargaining cases is limited to cover coerces, involuntary, or unknowing pleas of guilt. The right to appeal the facts of the case is a closed avenue to the defendant.

The plea bargaining process with all its associated problems has arisen because of other problems. The crowded courts, which the process circumvents, have arisen because of an increasing crime rate and a lack of financial resources. The problem of long pre-trial incarceration has been caused, in part, by the bail system. The rising crime rate has caused both prosecutors and public and private defense counsels to acquire cumbersome, if not totally unmanageable, workloads. The plea bargaining process has arisen as a resolution to these problems. It has proven its value to assist in the processing of large numbers of cases and assures conviction with minimum expense. It may also be maintaining the equilibrium in the criminal justice system.[59]

The current state of the criminal courts cannot survive the abolishment of plea bargaining unless it undergoes a major overhaul. A minimal 10 per cent reduction in the use of guilty pleas by the federal courts would double the number of trials.[60] An equivalent situation is experienced by state jurisdictions with crowded court dockets. Courts throughout the country have not kept pace with the growth of criminal caseloads. The United States Supreme Court in *Santobello v. New York* suggested that in order to provide each defendant with a full scale trial, the state and federal governments would be required to multiply by many times the number of judges and courts facilities. The plea bargaining system, however, needs standardized guidelines for negotiations with procedural guarantees and avenues of appeal for defendants which ensure their individual rights while simultaneously protecting society.[61]

Plea bargaining decisions should reflect policy, not the exercise of caprisious whim. Also, there should be equal justice under law, not arbitrary punishment of the weak.[62] The absence of consistency, equity, and openness of the plea bargaining process has led to an uneasiness regarding its extensive usage in the contemporary criminal procedures. It is the lack of public acceptance that has precipitated calls for the abolition of plea bargaining practices.[63]

When the concept of "justice" is evaluated by each offender answering for his actions it is difficult to determine how plea bargaining facilitates justice. In addition, plea bargaining causes the loss of public confidence in government, increases the likelihood of corruption in the prosecutor's office, negates the intent of the legislature, and permits poor bargains to be made through lack of experience or negligence of the prosecutors.[64] In these circumstances, neither the defendants who received a reduced sentence with a bargained guilty plea to an offense less than that which they actually committed or the innocent defendants who plead guilty have received justice. Society has a right to expect offenders to be convicted and punished to the extent the law allows. It also has the right to expect innocent individuals to be treated as such.[65] The plea bargaining process negates the expectations.

[1] *Harvard Law Review*. Plea bargaining and the transformation of the criminal process. (1977). p. 570.

[2] Kipnis, K. Criminal justice and the negotiated plea. *Ethics*. (1976). 86 (2) p. 93.

[3] Bond, J.E. *Bargaining and Guilty Pleas*. New York: Clark Boardman. (1975). p. 15-21 and Newman, D.J. *Conviction: The Determination of Guilt or Innocence Without Trial*. Boston, Ma: Little, Brown and Co., (1966). p. 220-221.

[4] Barbara, J., Morrison, J., and Cunningham, H., *Criminology*. (1976). 14 (1) p. 56; Cole, G.F. *The American System of Criminal Justice*. North Scitaute, Ma: Duxbury Co., (1975). p. 295; Green, T.S., Ward, J.D., and Arcuri, A. Plea bargaining fairness and inadequacy of representation. *Columbia Human Rights Law Review*. (1975). p. 496; and *Harvard Law Review*. The unconstitutionality of plea bargaining. (1970). p. 1389.

[5] Morley, R., The vanishing jury. *Southern California Law Review*. (1928). 2 (2) p. 96 and Wishingrad, J. The plea bargain in historical perspective. *Buffalo Law Review*. (1974). p. 508.

[6] Nagel, S.S., and Neff, M. The impact of plea bargaining on the judicial process. *American Bar Association Journal*. (1976) 62, p. 1020.

[7] Dean, J.M. Illegitimacy of plea bargaining.

Federal Probation. (1974) 38 (3). p. 20 and Newbauer, D.W. *America's Courts and the Criminal Justice System*. North Scituate, Ma: Duxbury Co., (1979). p. 309-310.

[8] President's commission on law enforcement and administration of justice. *The Challenge of Crime in a Free Society*. (1968) p. 333.

[9] Bechefsky, H.J., and Katkov, H.I. Another slant .... plea bargaining: an essential component of criminal justice. *California State Bar Journal*. (1977). 52. p. 214; and Kipnis, K. p. 95.

[10] Green, T. S., p. 497.

[11] United States Courts Annual Report: 1974. p. 402.

[12] Green, T.S., p. 497; Kress, J.M., The Agnew case: policy, prosecution and plea bargaining. *Criminal Law Bulletin*. (1974). 10. p. 82; President's commission, p. 33; and Thomas, E.S., Plea bargaining: the clash between theory and practice. *Loyola Law Review*. (1974). p. 303.

[13] There have been two predominate areas of plea negotiations. Charge bargaining has been the most widely accepted form of plea negotiations, but not necessarily the most appealing to the defendant. Sentence bargaining has been less prevalent and in most jurisdictions trial judges have been its chief proponents. In either form, plea negotiations have played a major role in the

daily operation and administration of justice and have become as common as committees in Congress. In addition, there are
two styles of plea bargaining agreements.
In the explicit bargain the prosecutor and
defense counsel discuss the terms of the
agreement which is both definite and legally binding, even though it may never be of-
ficially recorded. The tacit plea bargain
is generally not legally enforceable. The
agreement is made through intermediaries or
is inferred by the defendant from the behavior of the prosecutor. The defendant
may be advised by a third party that the
prosecutor will offer leniency in return
for a guilty plea. Subsequently, the defendant pleads guilty with the expectation,
but not the promise, of leniency. If their
expectations are unfounded the defendants
may be left embittered, but without legal
redress.

[14] Bond, J.E. Plea bargaining in North Carolina. *North Carolina Law Review*.
(1976). p. 840.

[15] Weinreb, L. *Denial of Justice*. New York:
Free Press Co., (1977). p. 71-72.

[16] Newbauer, D.W. After the arrest: the
charging decision in Prairie City. *Law
and Society Review*. (1974). p. 502.

[17] President's commission, p. 334.

[18] Lagoy, S., Senna, J., and Segal, L. An Empirical Study on information usage for prosecutorial decision making in plea negotia-

tions. *American Criminal Law Review*. (1976). p. 437.

[19] Newman, D., *Conviction*, p. 103.

[20] Cole, G., *American System*. p. 298.

[21] Inbau, F. *Cases and Comments on Criminal Procedure*. New York: Foundation Press. (1974). p. 486.

[22] Stein, S.L. Prosecutorial discretion and the initiation of criminal complaints. *Southern California Law Review*. (1969). p. 426.

[23] Lagoy, S., p. 437; and Wilson, J.Q. *Thinking About Crime*. New York: Basic Books. (1975). p. 179.

[24] Caplan, G., and Velde, R. *Prosecutorial Discretion: The Decision to Charge*. Washington, DC: National Criminal Justice Reference Service. (1975).

[25] Lagoy, S., p. 461.

[26] Dworkin, R.M. The model of rules. *University of Chicago Law Review*. (1967). p. 14.

[27] Douglas, J. *Discretionary Authority of the Prosecutor*. (1977). Houston: National College of District Attorneys. p. 1.

[28] Kuh, R.H. Sentencing: guidelines for the Manhattan District Attorney's Office. *Criminal Law Bulletin*. (1975). p. 58.

[29] Breitel, C.D. Controls in criminal law enforcement. *University of Chicago Law Review*. (1960). 27 (3). p. 427.

[30] Charge reduction is the inducement most frequently offered to the defendant by the prosecutor, which, in routine cases, automatically reduces the maximum possible sentence. In charge dismissal agreements one or more related charges are summarily dismissed. Subsequently, the defendant avoids the possibility of multiple convictions and extended sentences. Often prosecutors agree not to press additional criminal charges that could subject the defendant to more severe punishment under habitual offender statutes.

[31] In sentence recommendation agreements, the prosecutor submits a specific sentence to the judge. Unless the judge has been involved in the preliminary plea negotiations the recommendation is not binding on the court. However, following plea negotiations, judges usually accept the prosecutor's sentencing recommendations.

[32] *Blackledge v. Allison*, 97 S. Ct. 1621 (1977), *Brady v. United States*, 397 U.S. 742 (1970), *Santobello v. New York*, 404 U.S. 260 (1971).

[33] Miller, L.B. Judicial discretion to reject negotiated pleas. *Georgetown Law Journal*. (1974). p. 242.

[34] Miller, L., p. 244.

[35] Bubany, C., p. 483.

[36] Bond, J., *Bargaining*, p. 40; *Dewey v. United States*, 268 F. 2d 124 (8th Cir. 1959).

[37] *People v. Merchant*, 283 N.E. 2d 721 (Ill. 1972); *United States v. Stockwell*, 472 F. 2d 1186 (9th Cir. 1973).

[38] *Santobello v. New York*.

[39] *Poteet v. Fauver*, 517 F. 2d 393 (3rd Cir. 1975).

[40] Bond, J., *Bargaining*, p. 44.

[41] Weinreb, L., p. 75.

[42] Atkins, B., and Pogrebin, M. *The Invisible Justice System: Discretion and the Law*. Cincinnati, Oh: Anderson Publ. (1978). p. 5.

[43] Jacob, H. *Justice in America, Courts, Lawyers, and the Judicial Process*. New York: Foundation Press. (1974). p. 191.

[44] 97 S. Ct. 1621 (1977).

[45] 404 U.S. 260 (1971).

[46] Bond, J. *Bargaining*, p. 11-12; and Green, T., p. 498.

[47] 397 U.S. 742 (1970).

[48] 316 U.S. 101 (1942).

[49] 332 U.S. 708 (1948).

[50] 368 U.S. 487 (1962).

[51] Barbara, J., p. 60.

[52] Bubany, C., p. 480.

[53] Ibid., p. 481.

[54] Dean, J., p. 22.

[55] Remington, F., and Rosenblum, V. The criminal law and the legislative process. *University of Illinois Law Forum.* (1960). p. 495.

[56] Schmidt, E.F. Criminal procedure - plea bargaining - implicit restrictions. *Wayne Law Review.* (1975). p. 1162.

[57] 274 U.S. 220 (1927).

[58] Schmidt, E., p. 1162-1163.

[59] Cole, G.F. *Politics and the Administration of Justice*. Beverly Hills, Ca: Sage Publishing. (1973). p. 198.

[60] Burger, W. The state of the judiciary-1970. *American Bar Association Journal.* (1970). 56. p. 929.

[61] Remington, F., p. 499.

[62] Brietel, C., p. 430.

[63] Rosett, A., and Cressey, D. *Justice by*

Consent: *Plea Bargaining in the American Courthouse*. Philadelphia: J.B. Lippincott Publ. (1976). p. 5-7.

[64] Berger, M., p. 622-623.

[65] David, K.C. *Discretionary Justice*: *A Preliminary Inquiry*. Baton Rouge, La: Louisiana State University Press. (1969).

CAPITAL PUNISHMENT:
RECURRING ISSUES

A consistent consideration in the capital punishment controversy has been the perception of the threat of punishment; real or imagined. In reality, the identification of criminal offenders has been difficult and the rate of apprehension low. Also, it has been understandable why crime rates have consistently increased. The rate of criminal occurrances has increased while the corresponding rate of punishment has decreased.[1] In the past, this has been evidence of an increased opportunity to commit criminal acts or evidence of a society where the criminal justice system has displayed more interest in protecting the law violators than it has in protecting the victims.

Some citizens have felt that society has been as responsible for crime as the individuals who engage in criminal behavior. They believe punishment has been morally unjustified and ineffective in enforcing laws.[2] While society may have created a condition of anomie,[3] an individual must bear his own responsibility for criminal acts he has committed.

Although capital punishment has been discussed for generations, it remains one of the most critical issues in contemporary society. The issue has never been satisfactorily resolved. Following the execution of John Spenkelink on May 25, 1979, the capital punishment arguments resurfaced.

Capital Punishment in Perspective

In civilized societies, there have always been rules governing individual behavior. Throughout history no government has afforded total freedom to its citizens. In order for the individual to exercise maximum freedom the rights of others must be abridged. Thus, laws have been codified. Inherent in the laws have been warnings of the punishment which would be imposed if the laws were violated. Under the retributive perspective, when a person violated the law, they received that punishment which had been promised to him. If he was not punished, it has been assumed, he would continue to violate the law when the opportunity arose. If not the same law repeatedly, then others. Therefore, in order for the laws to remain effective, they must be enforced; if not, the individual will not heed them.

Capital punishment as a method for enforcing the law is not new. Capital punishment existed in the Code of Hamurrabi (1750 B.C.) which applied the death penalty for more than two dozen offenses, including: corruption in government service, sex offenses, and theft, but excluding murder. The Assyrian laws (1500 B.C.) prescribed the death penalty for numerous offenses, although other forms of punishment were more frequent.[4] Capital punishment in the Roman Empire was imposed for: arson, bearing false witness, bribery, murder, and treason. Similar to contemporary society, capital punishment under the Roman administration was unequally applied: execution was more common for "slaves" than for Roman "citizens". The Roman Code of Theodosius (438) specified over 80 offenses punishable by death.[5] In the 18th century, in England, there were approximately 160 offenses punishable by death.[6]

Colonial America utilized the death penalty extensively, however, capital offenses decreased after the American Revolution.[7] Also, the death penalty criteria has continuously changed after this period. For example, murder was first divided into degrees by Pennsylvania statute (1794) and it authorized capital punishment only for first degree murder. Michigan (1847) was the first state to abolish capital punishment for all offenses except treason.[8]

The execution of a human being has never been pleasant, however, the method of execution in contemporary America has not simulated the past inhumane methods of other societies: Ancient Rome,[9] China,[10] and France.[11]

The legal instrument of death in England, under the reign of Edward III (1334), was hanging. This method of execution remained part of English law and was incorporated into American law.[12] There were executions by hanging in the United States as recently as 1962, and several states have retained this method of execution.[13]

The New York State Legislature viewed electrocution as more humane than hanging and on August 6, 1890, in Auburn Prison, William Kemmler became the first person executed by electrocution in the United States.[14] This was followed by additional executions[15] by varying methods.[16]

Execution by poisonous gas was introduced in Nevada in 1924.[17] Despite the invention of the gas chamber, the majority of states provided for electrocution in their statutes.

In 1967, 41 states possessed capital punishment statutes and included murder as an offense requiring the death penalty. Many included kidnapping for ransom, but some qualified the penalty with circumstances where the victim was not released unharmed.[18] Following the decision in *Furman v. Georgia*,[19] the statutes of these states were ruled unconstitutional and, in effect, declared the application of existing capital punishment statutes unconstitutional. However, following *Gregg v. Georgia*[20] many states reinstated their capital punishment statutes, and in 1977, 35 states had capital punishment statutes.

Constitutionality of Capital Punishment

Early challenges of capital punishment have not directly addressed the constitutionality of the principle of capital punishment; their challenges were directed at the Eighth Amendment's perceived cruel and unusual aspects inherent in the method of execution employed in carrying out the sentence. For the crime of murder, *Wilkerson v. Utah*[21] established that a firing squad was not a cruel and unusual mode of imposing the death penalty. Wilkerson challenged the sentence of death by firing squad on the basis that the trial court had no statutory power to authorize the firing squad as the method of execution. In rejecting these arguments, the United States Supreme Court stated that while cruel and unusual punishments were forbidden by the Constitution, the punishment of death, i.e., execution by firing squad, was not included within those categories of punishment.[22] In further describing which categories of punishment were proscribed by the Eighth Amendment, the Supreme Court adopted the principle that punishments which involved torture and unnecessary cruelty were forbidden. The Supreme Court, however, has not articulated any criteria of what was unnecessarily cruel and unusual punishment.[23]

The United States Supreme Court first supported capital punishment in *In re Kemmler*.[24] The petitioner challenged the constitutionality of the method of execution, i.e., electrocution. The Supreme Court, in rejecting the petitioner's arguments, stated that punishments were cruel when they involved torture or a lingering death, but punishment of death was not cruel within the meaning of that word as used in the Constitution. Cruelty, therein, implied something inhumane and barbarous; something more than mere extinguishment of life.[25]

The principle of capital punishment was further separated from the method of execution in *Louisiana ex rel. Francis v. Resweber*.[26] The petitioner was convicted of murder and sentenced to death (by electrocution). The petitioner survived the attempted electrocution, presumably due to an equipment malfunction.[27] The Supreme Court ruled that a second attempt to execute the petitioner had not violated the cruelty against which the Constitution provided protection. A convicted offender's protection was against cruelty inherent in the method of punishment, not the necessary suffering involved in the method employed to extinguish life humanely. In *Francis v. Resweber* there was no intent to inflict unnecessary pain nor was there any unnecessary pain involved in the proposed execution. The United States Supreme Court concluded that the hardship imposed upon the petitioner had not risen to that level of hardship denounced as denial of due process due to cruelty.[28]

On the basis of *Wilkerson v. Utah*, *In re Kemmler*, and *Francis v. Resweber* it has been apparent that the United States Supreme Court has not disapproved the constitutionality of the concept of capital punishment. They have been slow, however, to identify criteria for applying the cruel and unusual proscription.

The arguments in *Furman v. Georgia* and its companion cases addressed the constitutionality of capital punishment.[29] However, the Court avoided enumerating the fundamental question of the Eighth Amendment's cruel and unusual clause and concluded that the Georgia statute, as applied, violated the Eighth and Fourteenth Amendments as being cruel and unusual punishment.[30]

In the concurring opinions in *Furman v. Georgia*[31] there were three distinct viewpoints represented. The first was directed toward the uncontrolled nature of the jury's discretion which could result in arbitrary and capricious imposition of the death penalty. One justice compared the probability of being sentenced to death with being struck by lightening.[32] The manner in which juries were perceived to have applied the death penalty was thought to be an impermissible system of justice.[33] This was supported by the fact that juries imposed death penalties so infrequently that the retribution justification for capital punishment has not been satisfied regardless of how much the defendant may have deserved death as a punishment.[34] If the underlying justification for the punishment was missing then there was no justification for imposing capital punishment. Similarly, the deterrence justification for capital punishment has not been served by the infrequent imposition of the death penalty. Common sense and experience has indicated that seldom-enforced laws become ineffective measures for controlling human conduct and that the death penalty, unless imposed with sufficient frequency, will make little contribution to deterrence.[35]

The infrequent imposition of capital punishment and uncontrolled jury discretion as a constitutional imperfection have conflicted with the decision in *McGautha v. California*, which concluded that a jury need not be provided with standards to guide its discretion in whether to recommend a sentence of death or life imprisonment.[36]

The second view was that the death penalty, as applied, in *Furman v. Georgia* was unconstitutional because it was employed in a discriminatory fashion. The attempt was made to establish that the use of capital punishment discriminated against various socio-economic and racial groups.[37]

The third view incorporated the influence of morality. The fact that death had been a rarely used form of punishment, became the basis for the rejection of the deterrence and retribution justifications.[38] Realistically, the concept of justice changes over time; and no immutable moral order has required death for murderers and rapists. However, society has desired to prevent crime, but society has not exhibited a desire to kill offenders simply to obtain revenge.[39]

Furman v. Georgia left the critical question unanswered; whether death, per se, was unconstitutional as a sanction for any crime under any circumstance. In addition, the *Furman v. Georgia* opinion provided only vague guidelines of how to meet the Eighth and Fourteenth Amendment requirements. However, the decision that the death penalty statute violated the cruel and unusual provisions of the Eighth and Fourteenth Amendments was not intended to extend beyond the statute as applied in *Furman*.[40]

The post-Furman legislation responded with two types of statutes: mandatory sentencing and guided jury discretion. Louisiana, for example, responded with the mandatory sentencing statute stating that

....whoever commits the crime of first degree murder shall be punished by death....[41] Under the Louisiana statute there was no jury discretion. However, the jury could impose the sentence of death on certain defendants while the mere conviction of other defendants mandated the sentence of death.

The guided jury discretion was utilized as an alternative to the mandatory sentencing statutes. The Georgia statute provided that upon trial by jury, a person convicted of an offense may be punishable by death. However, the sentence of death shall not be imposed unless the jury verdict included a finding of at least one statutory aggravating circumstance and a recommendation that the death sentence be imposed.[42]

The Georgia statute and procedure was intended to allow the jury to individualize the punishment of death only to those defendants who aggravated the circumstances of their offense in some way enumerated by the legislature. At the same time, this procedure allowed the jury to

- 142 -

spare the life of a guilty defendant if none of the statutory extras were present, or if mitigating factors dictated.[43] Both of these statutory plans were suggested in Chief Justice Burger's *Furman v. Georgia* dissent.[44]

The *Furman v. Georgia* decision concluded that the imposition of the death penalty was cruel and unusual because of its disparity in application.[45] The Supreme Court, in *Gregg v. Georgia* demonstrated that the death penalty in and of itself was neither cruel nor unusual. The suggested method to solve the problem of disparity in sentencing was to provide standards for juries and judges to follow when determining sentences.[46]

Two important issues have been resolved by *Furman v. Georgia*: first, capital punishment, per se, has not been violative of the Eighth and Fourteenth Amendments. Second, within the Eighth and Fourteenth Amendments which procedural mechanisms a state must utilize when imposing the death penalty for the crime of murder.[47] The constitutionality of capital punishment has been resolved in *Gregg v. Georgia*: capital punishment, per se, was not unconstitutional.[48] *Gregg v. Georgia* further resolved the procedural questions of how capital punishment could be constitutionally applied by validating the guided jury discretion statutes while overturning the mandatory sentencing statutes.[49]

Furman has been viewed as an anti-capital punishment decision, however, Gregg favored its retention. The abolitionists argue that society does not have the right to punish for the sake of retribution alone. However, the concept of retribution has not been the main objective of punishment, retribution has neither been forbidden or unwarranted.[50] Retribution has been and remains a basic right of all citizens, victims, and potential victims by seeking redress through appropriate government processes. Abolitionists have disclaimed the position that victims have legal and civil rights. They more often see the offender as the victim of society and the judicial system.

Morality and Justice in Capital Punishment

The constitutional issues have been crucial, however, their interpretation resides ultimately in the jurisdiction of the United States Supreme Court. Regardless of the constitutional interpretation, consideration must be afforded to the concepts of morality and justice associated with capital punishment. An argument against capital punishment has been presented because some guilty individuals have evaded punishment. This has allegedly occured because the guilty individuals were members of preferred groups noted for their social status, wealth, or occupational and political power. Whether this position has been accurate or not, it has been insufficient justification for permitting other guilty individuals to evade punishment. The counter-argument concluded that the allegation that some guilty individuals have evaded capital punishment supported extending its application to include them.

From the moral viewpoint the premeditated death of a human being is inexcusable, whether completed by the state or an individual. In addition, the application of the death penalty has raised the question of whether or not the power of the state should be used to extinguish human life; an action which has been a criminal violation under most circumstances when completed by individuals other than the state. Also, in reality, when speaking of convicted murderers, there have been practical problems of identifying those individuals. Legal processes entail considerable uncertainty and fallible human judgment has created the possibility of a fatal error in the application of the death penalty. Someone who should not, may be executed by the state.[51] In addition, the general deterrent defenses of capital punishment have not been supported by empirical research.[52] Homicide rates, for example, in states with and without capital punishment, show little cause and effect relationships.

The concept of justice has required the sanctioning of convicted offenders. In the current criminal justice bureaucracy, that has been interpreted to mean identifying, adjudicating, and sentencing as many law violators as humanly possible. The concept of justice applies even if only some of the guilty are punished, while simultaneously sparing as many of the innocent as possible, even if all have not been spared. The argument cannot logically be presented to treat everyone with equal injustice in preference to applying justice to some. Justice, therefore, cannot spare some guilty offenders or sanction some innocent offenders for the sake of equality on the premise that others have been unjustly spared or punished. In the reality of the criminal justice system, penalties can only be applied to the convicted individuals (those in custody) even though they cannot be equally applied to all other guilty individuals (those not apprehended). Morally, then, justice has been preferable to equality.[53]

The percentage of individuals receiving death sentences in comparison to all other sentences has been small, and the percentage of executions in comparison to the total number of individuals sentenced to death has been further limited.

Whether the death penalty, in its limited application, can be considered morally justified has been a prime issue. This has been the essential moral issue, as separated from the constitutional and justice arguments. If the death penalty were applied to all convicted offenders in capital cases, but considered morally unjustified, then even though equally applied, the penalty would be unjustified in each case. However, if the death penalty was morally justified, even though discriminatorily applied to only some of the convicted offenders, then the death penalty remains justified in each case to which it was applied. Discrimination based on sex, race or socio-economic class becomes irrelevant to the moral question. The basis for supportive argument has been the fact that a higher percentage of males, poor,[54] or blacks[55] have been found guilty of capital offenses; more than women, wealthy individuals, or caucasions. Discrimination alone has not invalidated capital punishment. Discrimination by sex, race, or social class has contributed to a system of unequal justice.

The utilitarian effects of unequal justice have been generally detrimental to the social structure because the unequal application of punishment offends the individual's sense of justice. Unequal justice has also been morally objectionable. However, unequal justice is still justice. The guilty do not become inno-

cent or less deserving of punishment because
others have evaded punishment. No one has argued that any innocent indivudial deserved punishment because others were punished. That position would lack equity and justice
simultaneously, where applied. Basically, justice remains just, however unequal; while injustice remains unjust, regardless of how well intended or equally applied. Justice and
equality, then, are not identical nor inter-
changeable, but both have been desired. Equality in the eyes of the law should be extended and
enforced; however, not at the expense of justice.

Anti-capital punishment arguments based on
religion have reinforced their arguments with
passages from the scripture: ".... an eye for an
eye...."[56] and the Sixth Commandment, "Thou
shalt not kill."[57] The "eye for an eye" passage was contradicted in philosophy when Jesus
advised his followers "to turn the other
cheek."[58] The Bible has generally been subjected to broad interpretations, but primarily
Jesus stated that he came not to destroy the
law, but to fulfill it.[59]

The Bible provided specific reference to
capital punishment wherein "....if a man spills
innocent blood by innocent blood his blood shall
be spilled."[60] In addition, the Bible has supported the delineation between premeditated murder and manslaughter.[61]

In biblical times, God gave the Israelites,
as a nation, a set of rules to govern their
lives. Included in these rules were directives
toward instituting and utilizing the death penalty. Death was presecribed for: adultery,[62]
blasphemy,[63] disobedience to parents,[64] in-

cest,[65] rape,[66] sodomy,[67] the teaching of
false doctrines,[68] and witchcraft.[69]

Those who favor the abolition of capital
punishment based on the religious standpoint
have relied on the aspect of forgiveness. God
has forgiven those who have repented, but God
also has been just. Though God has forgiven, he
has not allowed individuals to escape the consequences of what they have done. For example,
David,[70] whom God favored, was chastened; and
the thief on the cross whom Christ forgave, but
was not removed from the crucifiction cross.[71]
God has not removed all pain and suffering of
consequences during forgiveness.

The Effectiveness of Capital Punishment

Deterrence
Considerable research has been devoted to
general deterrence rather than to specific deterrence; yet, in general, deterrence has not
been accurately measured. The deterrence effect
cannot be determined as to how many people have
not committed a crime because of fear of certain
punishment as opposed to other factors.

Caesar Becarria[72] maintained that it was
the certainty of the punishment which deterred
rather than the severity.[73] This principle has
been critical when considering that for more
than 60 per cent of all felonies, there have
been no arrests. Also, less than 1 per cent of
those arrested have been tried; the remainder of
arrestees have been released or the charges plea
bargained.[74] As certainty and severity have
been applied to capital punishment, for example,
the state of Ohio executed an average of one out

of 116 persons who committed non-negligent homicide. One out of 1.3 offenders admitted to Ohio institutions under the sentence of death were actually executed.[75]

The most vocal arguments against capital punishment have been that there has not been significant evidence that it has acted as a deterrent. Numerous studies have consisted of comparisons between the murder rates in states which have capital punishment and states which do not; without considering the rate of apprehension, conviction, or the actual use of the death penalty.[76] Also, studies have been based on the eight states which abolished capital punishment and then reinstated it, but have not considered other influential factors that fluxuated during the years between abolition and reinstatement. Therefore, these studies have lacked the depth and reliability required before formulating concrete conclusions.

One study concluded that, with reference to homicide, the greater the certainty and severity, the lower the homicide rates.[77] Though research has been conducted in this area, and many have aligned themselves on both sides of the argument, no study to date has satisfactorily proven that there was or was not a relationship between legal sanctions and criminal occurrences. The research has not addressed all the variables to adequately assess the question. It has been difficult, if not impossible, to isolate the relationship between the crime rate and the severity and certainty of punishment from factors such as the socio-economic background of a community, population patterns, and factors which affect the perceived severity and certainty. Within this perception of severity and certainty, there has been an infinite number of variables which vary with the individual being deterred (or remaining undeterred.)

However, certainty without severity has been as ineffective as the lack of certainty. There has been no rational reason why an individual would be deterred from committing an offense when their offense would bring possible satisfaction with the potential risk of penalty being small by comparison. In the cost-benefit analysis, it has been perceived to be worth their effort to behave as they wish in spite of the fact that they may have to pay a relatively small fee. It has also been apparent that many individuals in the society have been willing to gamble on apprehension, conviction, and sentencing to a few years in prison to have what they want, but are they willing to gamble on death? The abolitionists argue that a life sentence is no small fee; however, it has been a normal procedure that life sentences have been merely a given number of years before parole was granted.

The initial advocation of certainty without severity resulted from the conditions of the prisons at the time, or concern that resulted from the severity of penalties, which were unequally applied.[78] However, the problems of unequal application of punishments remains today. In the debate over capital punishment the issue should not be whether or not the death penalty deters, but rather whether or not it has been a more effective deterrent than its alternative.[79]

The accepted alternative to the death penalty has been life imprisonment. There have been a few people who believed that life imprisonment was worse than capital punishment. One study reported that 55.7 per cent of inmates sentenced to life imprisonment considered that fear of the death penalty had not prevented crime, while 28.1 per cent of the non-life sentenced inmates agreed; 41.5 per cent of these inmates strongly agreed that the death penalty was the worst possible punishment, 22 per cent agreed, 14.6 disagreed, and 15.4 strongly disagreed.[80]

The reality of life imprisonment has been that, although some prisoners have died (prematurely) in prison before their life sentence had been served, no one has spent the remainder of his natural life in prison.[81] The majority of state statutes delineating life imprisonment have accounted for this phenomena.[82]

Those who deny that deterrence exists, have done so on the basis that crimes continue to be committed. Retentionists have not claimed that all individuals will be deterred. There does not have to be a 100 per cent or even a 90 per cent deterrence from crime in order for the possibility of the deterrence effect to exist. To follow this line of reasoning has suggested, the conclusion could be the opposite; i.e., since the majority of citizens have not committed crimes, it can be concluded that there has been a deterrence effect.

A comparison of jurisdictions with similar characteristics: cultural, social, and economic, but varied statutes on capital punishment reported little or no statistical evidence of a deterrence effect.[83] However, the lack of statistical evidence for a deterrence effect has not automatically verified a non-deterrence effect. It merely has shown the lack of statistical evidence in favor of a deterrence factor.[84]

There have been contrary indications in cases where offenders were arrested and stated that they would have killed someone, but were deterred because of fear of the death penalty. Some had even carried toy pistols or otherwise simulated possession of a weapon during robberies because they feared accidentally shooting someone and being sentenced to death.[85]

One fact remains, the number of homocides doubled in the past decade; the years between the executions of Luis Monge in 1967 and Gary Gilmore in 1977. This has indicated that, while the death penalty has statistically shown little or no deterrence effect, not having it has been less.[86]

The research on general deterrence has been inadequate when measuring fear as a potent control of human behavior and few fears have been more powerful than the fear of death. Further, whatever the general deterrence effect on the behavior of others, the execution of a convicted murderer, with 100 per cent certainty, deters that person. For some, to have evaded legal sanctions has distorted the concept of justice.

Rehabilitation

The reality that capital punishment voids the possibility of rehabilitation has been a prime argument for abolition. This has been true, however, rehabilitation has seldom been effective. Rehabilitation depends on many variables, most of which have been involved in the psychological and emotional makeup of the offender. While some rehabilitation programs have reported a relatively low rate of recidivism there have been cases where a murderer was on parole when he was charged with additional homicides.[87] Also, society has encountered some individuals that actually enjoy killing people.[88]

Generally, efforts to rehabilitate offenders have only limited success. One study of 150 murderers reported that they had not committed additional homicides and only two had committed other crimes. The study concluded that murderers were no threat to the public.[89] Contrary to these studies and conclusions, there were numerous cases of murderers who, upon their release from prison, killed again.[90] In these instances it has not been logical to suggest that these specific multivictim murderers be released again to resume their murderous activities.

To the contrary, it has been suggested that the execution of one offender has the potential of saving the lives of eight victims.[91] Though these studies come under criticism, when they involved the lives of innocent citizens, society simply cannot discount the possibility of the results being valid. Also, due to parole practices and the possibilities of escape, there have been no other mechanisms to insure that there will be no second or third murders except to execute the offender.

The Potential Miscarriage of Justice

The average citizen cannot imagine committing an act so horrible that they would be jeopardized by capital punishment. However, they have been exposed to the media news reports and know that the average citizen stands a greater chance of being murdered on the streets, or even in their homes, than being subjected to capital punishment. One study revealed that the average citizen statistically stands a greater chance of being murdered by a felon than that of a combat soldier being killed on the battlefield during World War II.[92]

Abolitionists have argued that there has been a chance for a miscarriage of justice by permitting an innocent person to be executed, but provided very little consideration to a possible mistake in the opposite direction which could result in one life or many innocent lives being lost.

Sentencing Disparity

The argument has been made that capital punishment should be abandoned due to the disparity of sentencing. There has been sentencing disparity and many injustices have arisen, not only from disparity of sentencing, but also from the different quality of attorneys representing offenders and actual treatment and consideration given to them.[93] However, it is the disparity which has required change and improvement, not the death penalty. The punishment of death should not depend upon race, sex, age, education or financial ability to secure a competent attorney.[94] It should depend solely upon the crime and its attendant circumstances.

Cost Effectiveness

It has been suggested that the cost of capital punishment has been far more expensive than life imprisonment. This perspective considered the expense involved in selecting juries, trial costs and employee salaries, and continued expenses through all of the appeals processes when the sentence of death was imposed. In addition, there have been the costs of housing the offender in maximum security while the trial or appeals have progressed; through stays of execution, to the final date of commutation or of execution.[95]

Public Opinion

The infrequent utilization of capital punishment has been interpreted to mean that it reflected the popular distaste for executions. This conjecture has been partly based upon the Furman decision and hope that the American people were supporting the abolitionist's position.[96]

The infrequent imposition of capital punishment has reflected judicial caution, not distaste. Capital punishment was never intended for "all" offenders; it was intended to be used with caution and imposed when the judicial authorities were convinced that the offender was guilty of the crime for which death was provided as a penalty. Popular opinion, in three states: California, Illinois, and Washington, has suggested that capital punishment was generally supported. In all three states the vote was 2 to 1 to retain or restore capital punishment.[97]

It has been suggested that if the average citizen knew more about capital punishment, the evidence would convince them that it was immoral.[98] On the contrary, if they knew more about capital punishment, it would serve more readily as a measurable deterrent.

A bitter truth has become apparent, if capital punishment has not in fact been a deterrent, the worst that society has done has been to execute convicted murderers.[99] And, it has been better to execute convicted murderers than to take the chance of those or additional murderers taking the lives of other innocent victims.

In conclusion, when reviewing capital punishment it is disturbing to discover that a greater emphasis is placed on the offender than on the unsuspecting victim. There is evidence of a growing attitude toward discarding the victims and concentrating on the offenders. This is not totally irrational, the victims remain dead, they are eliminated from society forever. There is nothing that can be done to ease the suffering or pain of the victim, this is true; however, they should not have met their premature demise in vain, and all possible efforts must be made to protect the next potential victim. This is not an idle suggestion. People describe how inhumane and cruel capital punishment is, not only to the offender but the immediate relatives.[100] But this is true for the victims as well, a homicide victim may leave a spouse, children, or assorted relatives who depend upon them for support. The crime of homicide touches many people beside the immediate victim and offender. The social values are reversed in this circumstance; it is the murders of innocent and unsuspecting people that should be considered cruel and inhumane; not the execution of convicted murderers.

[1] Zimring, Franklin E., and Hawkins, Gordon J. *Deterrence: The Legal Threat in Crime Control*. Chicago: University of Chicago Press, 1973, p. 336.

[2] Van den Haag, Ernest. *Punishing Criminals*. New York: Basic Books, Inc., 1975, p. 6.

[3] Durkeim, Emile. *The Division of Labor in Society*. New York: The Free Press, 1964; Merton, Robert K. *Social Theory and Social Structure*. New York: The Free Press, 1968, p. 190, 192-193.

[4] Sills, David (ed.). *International Encyclopedia of the Social Sciences*. New York: McMillan Company, 1968, p. 290.

[5] Ibid., p. 291.

[6] Ibid.

[7] Ibid., p. 292.

[8] Ibid.

[9] Bishop, George V. *Executions, The Legal Ways of Death*, Los Angeles: Sherbourne Press, Inc., 1965, p. 67, 70.

[10] Ibid., p. 145.

[11] Ibid., p. 105.

[12] Ibid.

[13] Ibid., p. 110.

[14] Ibid., p. 17-21.

[15] Ibid., p. 24-25.

[16] Ohio Legislative Service Commission. *Capital Punishment*. Columbus, Oh.: Ohio Legislative Service Commission, January 1961, #46, p. 26.

[17] Bishop, p. 163.

[18] Bedau, Hugo A. "The Laws, the Crimes, and the Executions," Hugo A. Bedau (ed.) *The Death Penalty in America: An Anthology*. Garden City, NY: Doubleday and Co., Inc., 1967, p. 32-49.

[*19*] 408 U.S. 239 (1972).

[*20*] 428 U.S. 153 (1976).

[*21*] 99 U.S. 130 (1878).

[22] 99 U.S. 130, 134-135 (1878).

[23] 99 U.S. 130 (1878).

[*24*] 136 U.S. 436 (1890).

[25] 136 U.S. 436, 447 (1890).

[*26*] 329 U.S. 459 (1947).

[27] 329 U.S. 459, 469 (1947).

[28] 329 U.S. 459, 464 (1947).

[29] 225 Ga. 253, 167 S.E. 2d 618 (1969); *Jack-*

son v. *Georgia* 225 Ga. 790, 171 S.E. 2d 501 (1969); *Branch* v. *Texas* 447 S.W. 2d 932 (Tex. Crim. 1969).

[30] *Furman* v. *Georgia* 408 U.S. 238, 239-240 (1972).

[*31*] 408 U.S. 238, 240 Justice Douglas; at 257 Justice Brennan; at 306 Justice Stewart; at 310 Justice White; at 314 Justice Marshall (1972).

[32] *Furman* v. *Georgia* 408 U.S. 238, 309-310 Justice Stewart (1972).

[33] 408 U.S. 238, 310 (1972).

[34] 408 U.S. 238, 311 (1972).

[35] 408 U.S. 238, 312 (1972).

[36] 402 U.S. 183, 196 (1971).

[37] *Furman* v. *Goergia* 408 U.S. 238, 249-251 Justice Douglas; at 356-366 Justice Marshall (1972).

[38] 398 U.S. 238, 296 Justice Brennan; at 316-328 Justice Marshall (1972).

[39] 408 U.S. 238, 304-305 (1972).

[*40*] 408 U.S. 238, 239-240 (1972).

[41] L.A. Rev. Stat. Ann. para 14:30 (ammended 1973).

[42] Georgia Code Ann. para 26-3102 (1977

Supp.).

[43] *Furman v. Georgia* 408 U.S. 238, 400-401, (1972).

[44] 408 U.S. 238, 401 (1972).

[45] Carrington, Frank G., *Neither Cruel nor Unusual*. New Rochelle, NY: Arlington House Pub., 1978, p. 168.

[46] Carrington, p. 176.

[47] *Gregg v. Georgia* 428 U.S. 153 (1976); *Proffitt v. Florida* 428 U.S. 242 (1976); *Jurek v. Texas* 428 U.S. 262 (1976); *Woodson v. North Carolina* 428 U.S. 280 (1976); *Roberts v. Louisiana* 428 U.S. 325 (1976).

[48] 428 U.S. 153, 169 (1976).

[49] 428 U.S. 153, 163 (1976).

[50] Carrington, p. 136-137.

[51] Black, Charles L., *Capital Punishment: The Inevitability of Caprice and Mistake*. New York: Norton Co., 1974.

[52] Bailey, William C., "Murder and the Death Penalty", *Journal of Criminal Law and Criminology* 65 (1974), p. 416; Bailey, William C., "Murder and Capital Punishment", *American Journal of Orthopsychiatry* (1975), p. 669-688; Baldus, David C., and Cole, James W.L., "A Comparison of the Work of Thorsten Sellin and Isaac Ehrlich on the Deterrent Effect of Capital Punishment",

Yale Law Review 85 (1975), p. 170-186; Bedau, Hugo A., and Pierce, Chester M., (eds.) *Capital Punishment in the United States*. New York: AMS Press, 1976; Bowers, William J., *Executions in America*. Lexington, MA: Lexington Books, 1975; Gibbs, Jack P., *Crime, Punishment and Deterrence*. New York: Elsevier, 1975; Sellin, Thorsten, *The Death Penalty*. Philadelphia: Executive Office, American Law Institute, 1959; Zimring and Hawkins, 1973.

[53] Van den Haag, Ernest, "In Defense of the Death Penalty: A Legal-Practical-Moral Analysis" *Criminal Law Bulletin* 14 (1978), p. 51-68.

[54] Diamond, Bernard L., "Murder and the Death Penalty: A Case Report" *American Journal of Orthopsychiatry* 45 (1975), p. 712; Solomon, George F., "Capital Punishment as Suicide and as Murder" *American Journal of Orthopsychiatry* 45 (1975), p. 701.

[55] Riedel, Marc, "Discrimination in the Imposition of the Death Penalty: A Comparison of the Characteristics of Offenders Sentenced Pre-Furman and Post-Furman" *Temple Law Quarterly* 49 (1976), p. 261.

[56] Exodus 21:24.

[57] Ibid., 20:13.

[58] Matthew 5:39.

[59] Ibid., 5:17,18.

[60] Genesis 9:5-6.

[61] Deuteronomy 19:4; 19:11, 12, 13.

[62] Leviticus 20:10.

[63] Ibid., 24:11-16, 23.

[64] Deuteronomy 21:18-21.

[65] Leviticus 20:11-14.

[66] Deuteronomy 22:25.

[67] Leviticus 20:13.

[68] Deuteronomy 13:1-10.

[69] Exodus 21:18.

[70] II Samuel 11:1-27; 12:1-14; 12:15-23.

[71] Luke 24:42, 43.

[72] Carrington, p. 19.

[73] Becarria, Caesar Bonesarra Marquis, *An Essay on Crimes and Punishment*. Stanford: Academic Reprints, 1953, p. 93.

[74] Van den Haag, p. 158.

[75] Approximately one out of five offenders subject to indictment for criminal homicide were charged with first degree murder and thereby subject to capital punishment. One out of four offenders admitted to Ohio institutions convicted of first degree murder

were admitted under sentence of death. Ohio Legislative Service Commission, 1961, p. 50.

[76] Andenaes, Johannes, "General Prevention Revisited: Research and Policy Implications." *Journal of Criminal Law and Criminology* 66 (1975) p. 338-365; Gibbs, Jack P., *Crime, Punishment, and Deterrence*. New York: Elseview, 1975; Erickson, Maynard and Gibbs, Jack P., "Further Findings on the Deterrence Question and Strategies for Further Research." *Journal of Criminal Justice* 4 (Fall 1976), p. 175-189; Meier, Robert D., "The Deterrence Doctrine and Public Policy: A Response to Utilitarians." James Cramer (ed.), *Preventing Crime*. Beverly Hills, Ca: Sage Publ., 1978, p. 233-247.

[77] Van den Haag, p. 137.

[78] Ibid., p. 115.

[79] Zimring and Hawkins, p. 14.

[80] This compares with 39.6 of the non-life sentenced inmates who strongly agreed, 20.7 per cent agree, 17.2 per cent disagreed and 14.5 per cent strongly disagreed. It would seem that a person convicted of murder in the first degree deserves the "worst" possible punishment, and if inmates feel the worst penalty is the death penalty, even if they do not feel it deters them, or do not admit that it failed to deter them, then that is the punishment that should be imposed. Certainly, they would not be more deterred by a penalty which they do not

feel is less than the maximum. Commonwealth of Pennsylvania, Department of Justice, Bureau of Correction, *Inmate Attitudes Toward the Death Penalty*. July,
1977, p. 25-29.

[81] Jayewardene, C.H.S., *The Penalty of Death*,
Lexington, Ma: D.C. Heath and Co., 1977, p.
88.

[82] For example, Section 2965.23 of the Ohio
Revised Code established the basic terms of
eligibility for parole for all sentences
exceeding 15 years. This section requires
the Pardon and Parole Commission to conduct
a hearing to consider a recommendation of
communtation after an offender has served a
minimum of 20 years of a life sentence for
first degree murder. Any inmate serving a
sentence exceeding 15 years for other than
first degree murder or treason becomes eli-
gible for parole after ten years. Ohio
Legislative Service Commission, 1961, p.
80.

[83] Sellin, Thorsten. "Death and Imprisonment
as Deterrent to Murder," Hugo A. Bedau
(ed.), *The Death Penalty in America*: *An
Anthology*. Garden City, NY: Doubleday and
Co., 1967, p. 284.

[84] Carrington, p. 89.

[85] Ibid., p. 93-94.

[86] Ibid., p. 76.

[87] Samuels, Gertrude. "Parole: The Issue and

the Promise," Grant S. McClellan (ed.),
Capital Punishment. New York: H.W. Wilson
Co., 1961, p. 34.

[88] Carrington, p. 29-30.

[89] McNamara, Donal J., "Statement Against Cap-
ital Punishment," Hugo A. Bedau (ed.)
The Death Penalty in America. Garden
City, NY: Doubleday and Co., 1967, p. 192.

[90] Carrington, p. 109-110.

[91] Erlich, Isaac. "The Deterrent Effect of
Capital Punishment," *American Economic
Review* (June 1975), p. 397-417.

[92] Carrington, p. 54.

[93] Chessman, Caryl. *Cell 2455 Death Row*.
Englewood Cliffs, NJ: Prentice-Hall, Inc.
1954; Wolfe, Burton H. *Pile-Up on Death
Row*. Garden City, NY: Doubleday and Co.,
1973.

[94] Wall Street Journal, November 1, 1978, p.
1.

[95] Nakell, Barry. "The Cost of the Death Penalty," *Criminal Law Bulletin* 14 (January-
February, 1978) 1, p. 69-80.

[96] McNamara, p. 183.

[97] Carrington, p. 59.

[98] Berkson, Larry C. *The Concept of Cruel
and Unusual Punishment*. Lexington,

Mass.: D.C. Heath and Co., 1975, p. 47.

[99] Carrington, p. 77.

[100] Wolfe, p. 65.

LAW AND ETHICS: WATERGATE

When the first White House transcripts were released in May, 1974, it was widely asserted that they showed the White House was occupied by men of cheap and sleazy character.[1]

Conservative Republican Congressman H.R. Gross of Iowa said the transcripts showed "an amazing lack of social sensitivity in the Office of the Presidency.[2] And Senator Packwood of Oregon found Richard M. Nixon's view of the government "frightening" because "there are not even token cliches about what is good for the people."[3]

One might conclude from these sorts of comments that Richard M. Nixon, President of the United States, and the men, especially the lawyers, who surrounded him, were without any ideals whatsoever. And the frightening spectre of Watergate might press one to argue that bar associations should increase their emphasis on presentation of "just causes"; that lawyers should be trained to have moral ideals; that they should be required to represent causes in which they believe and reject employment from clients who, in their judgment, are immoral.

One would argue then that Watergate happened because the John Deans, the John Mitchells, the John Erlichmans, the Herbert Kalmbachs were wrong because they were, in effect, on the wrong side.

But, for the pupose of argument at least, I will disagree. I will argue that pursuance of the above argument is a disservice to the legal profession. I will argue that, in fact, the lawyers involved in Watergate, who were either indicted or whose reputation was tarnished, were men of what they at least considered high moral cause, and that, on the other side, the attorneys whose reputations were enhanced by their performance in Watergate cases were essentially "hired guns",[4] men without ideals other than "zealous representation of their clients within the law."[5]

I intend to make the argument on empirical grounds by describing the actions of selected lawyers based on information in the public record. I think that it will become quite clear that the attorneys who emerged as "ethical" were, at the same time, "hired guns" with little personal bias toward the cause of their client, and that the men who emerged as "unethical" were victims of an overwhelming committment to a cause, whether that cause is considered a man, an institution or an idealogy.

The implication of such an argument concerns the historical ethical dilemma facing the attorney-at-law as stated in this instance by Weckstein:

> The emphasis upon the professional role of the lawyer and the responsibilties implicit in such a role, posits the issue of how the lawyer is to resolve conflicts which may develop between his role as an officer of the court and his moral responsibilities as a human being and a concerned citizen.[6]

Younger lawyers have a tendency to say that the dilemma to be solved is frequently on the side of the lawyer's responsibilities as a human being and a concerned citizen.

The purpose of this chapter is to show that when a lawyer is acting especially as an officer of the court, the dilemma must almost necessarily be solved on the side of the law, even if the law conflicts with his sense of responsibilities as a human being and a concerned citizen.

This chapter is organized according to attorneys and the various roles they play in regard to Citizen Richard M. Nixon and Richard M. Nixon, President of the United States. We begin with a discussion of Nixon followed by the Attorney General's office and discuss John Mitchell, Richard Kleindeinst, and Henry Petersen; followed by Citizen Nixon's Personal Attorney Herbert M. Kalmbach and his special attorney for Watergate related court actions, James St. Clair; followed by the Watergate prosecutor, Leon Jaworski, who though technically under the aegis of the Justice Department, came to act independently and more as an agent of the court and of Congress.

Citizen Nixon vs. the President of the United States.

Whether one discusses Richard M. Nixon from a philosophical, psychological, or legal point of view, it is impossible to avoid the very clear identification of himself with the President of the United States.

Even in the early stages of his presidency, Nixon frequently spoke of himself in the third person - as the president, as "he", but almost never as "Nixon."[7]

Nixon the man had a keen sense of his "ene-mies", typically the press, liberals and Demo-crats, the New Left, increasingly the Congress. The famous "enemies list" is symptomatic of his sense of being in a constant battle, and as his presidency progressed and his Watergate troubles increased, the mythical enemies list grew.

Early on in his Watergate troubles, in a conversation with Dean and Haldeman, Nixon said, "Just remember the trouble we are taking, we'll have a chance to get back one day..."[8]

Later in the same discussion, he said, re-ferring to the election campaign and disclosures of the Watergate break-in:

> We are all in it together. This is a war. We take a few shots and it will all be over. Don't worry. I wouldn't want to be on the other side right now.[9]

At this point, Dean says he has been taking notes on certain White House enemies, and Nixon amplifies:

> I want the most comprehensive notes on all those who tried to do us in. They didn't have to do it. They are asking for it and they are going to get it. We have not used the power in this first four years as you know. We have not used the Bureau (FBI) and we have not used justice, but things are going to change now. And they are either going to do it right or go.[10]

Before the Watergate Committee, Dean quotes Nixon as threatening to fire George Schultz, the

Secretary of the Treasury, for not cooperating with a White House plan to punish the 500 enemies on its list: Nixon said, according to Dean, "If George Schultz thinks he's some sort of candy-ass over this (the crackdown on 'enemies'), tell me and I'll get him out."[11]

The Nixon list of enemies apparently grew to include all but his most trusted advisors. During his tenure in office, the White House staff grew from 250 to 510 as more and more decision-making power became centered in the White House and away from ordinary cabinet departments. Foreign policy was conducted in the basement of the White House by Henry Kissinger and his staff, the budgetary functions were drawn into the White House, and "overlordships were created in each major area of government" with all the wires leading directly into the White House.[12] The object of this White House expansion was to focus all decision-making in the White House and away, especially, from bureaucracies, which became a Nixon enemy. As New York magazine stated, it also spared Nixon human contact "which he found so uncongenial" by focusing most of his contact on Halderman, Erlichman, Mitchell, and later John Connally.[13]

By focusing this power in the White House, Nixon succeeded, in some sense, in rubbing this atmosphere off on his aides, who became equally embroiled in a battle. Tom Huston, an aide who authored an extensive surveillance plan later vetoed by FBI director J. Edgar Hoover, testified before the Senate Watergate Committee that, "No one who had been in the White House could help but feel he was in a state of siege."[14]

Nixon apparently had succeeded in creating in himself an image beyond that of even the President. Hugh Sloan testified, "There was no independent sense of morality there .... if you worked for someone, he was God and whatever the orders were, you did it, it was all so narrow, so closed."[15]

But the initial sense of identification of Richard M. Nixon as "the President" went futher. As the peril to his own tenure as President increased, he began to identify *his* presidency as the Office of the Presidency. His personal lawyer, at one point, actually said he was representing the "Office of the Presidency"[16] and later, under pressure, softened the statement.

This merging of identities reached its peak stage in the defense case for the *United States v. Richard M. Nixon, President of the United States.[17]*

The defense case, organized by Nixon's attorney St. Clair, probably reflected Nixon's state of mind. It rested on two planks which had they been upheld by the Supreme Court, would have effectively identified the Office of the Presidency with the government of the United States (this despite the fact that the government was legally Nixon's adversary).[18]

St. Clair would argue that 1) the Court lacked jurisdiction in the matter of deciding whether Nixon should surrender Presidential tapes based on the contention that the President was the nation's "chief law enforcement" officer with final authority over who to prosecute and with what evidence; 2) that the President controlled the Justice Department; and 3) that the Special Prosecutor, being part of the Justice Department, was subordinate to him; and that therefore this was an intra-branch dispute within the Executive Branch.[19]

The argument was a reasonably clear attempt to place the Presidency "beyond the law." In questioning by Justice Thurgood Marshall, St. Clair left the matter of Nixon's compliance with a Court ruling up in the air; "This is being submitted to this court for its guidance and judgment. The President, on the other hand, has his obligations under the Constitution."[20]

The argument was a somewhat veiled assertion that Nixon might still consider himself exempt from court action and certainly from the law.

In its ruling on the justiciability of the case, the Court held first that "the mere assertion of a claim of 'intra-branch dispute', without more, has never operated to defeat federal jurisdiction (II, 8, 9). Noting that the case concerned evidence sought for a criminal violation of federal statutes, the Court noted that Congress had vested in the Attorney General the power to conduct criminal litigation and to appoint subordinates to assist him. And the Court noted that pursuant to its duties, the Attorney General appointed a Special Prosecutor "with explicit power to contest the invocation of executive privilege....[21] The Court continued, "So long as this regulation is extant, it has the force of law."[22]

In this instance, the Court noted the uniqueness of this particular prosecutor: the Attorney General could not remove the Special Prosecutor "without the consensus of eight designated leaders of Congress.[23]

Possibly in reference to Nixon's claim that he was, in some sense, "beyond the law," the Court noted that not only the Executive Branch, but the United States as the sovereign composed of three branches is bound to "respect and enforce" the regulation.[24]

On the second claim, St. Clair argued that Nixon had an absolute claim to executive privilege, that only he could decide which conversations to make public, and not the courts.[25]

St. Clair argued that the claim was absolute, even in the case of "criminal conspiracy," which he claimed could not be considered criminal until it was proven criminal, in order to assure the President a flow of "free and untrammeled information."[26]

The claim, if upheld, would have made the President the final arbiter of which evidence to release in a criminal conspiracy. Not incidentally, the claim would have violated both the New Code of Professional Responsibility and the old Canon of Ethics, with respect to an attorney's duty to report to the courts any evidence of a criminal conspiracy.

According to the two claims, the President would be exempt from the Code of Professional Responsibility. Such an exemption would not necessarily be bad, except that the President's claim to be the "chief law enforcement official" would make the argument specious.

In its judgment, the Court exercised great care to avoid limiting the executive privilege claim with respect to military and diplomatic matters, but held that "The impediment that unqualified privilege would place in the way of the primary Constitutional duty of the Judicial Branch to do justice in criminal prosecutions would plainly conflict with the function of the courts under Article III, (IV, 36). The Court then returned to the purpose of the framers of the Constitution in organizing the three branches of government, which the Court said "were not intended to operate with absolute independence."[27]

In both instances, the Court plainly took care to point out that the President was not "beyond the law," at least with reference to criminal proceedings, and repeatedly insisted that the United States as sovereign was composed of three branches of government, and that those branches did not operate in isolation of each other.

While such arguments were immediately obvious to even those who were not legal scholars, it was equally clear that President Richard M. Nixon was not operating within that framework.[28]

Nixon did operate with increasing isolation not only from Congress, but increasingly from his own executive branch and cabinet department, and it was a fairly logical outgrowth for him to argue that he was also isolated, and therefore exempt from the judiciary.

Nixon did not operate within the Constitution, nor within the principles of law. It is difficult to say that he operated within some positive idealogy. More effective cases have been made that Nixon was not an idealogue, but a pragmatist.

Nixon himself, even in the later days of Watergate, thought of himself as the supreme pragmatist: "My strong point, if I have a strong point, is that I always produce more than I promise....[29] I believe in playing politics hard, but I am also smart."[30]

There are ironies in all of these statements. Nixon may have played politics hard, but at least in his second term, he played it incredibly stupid. His second injunction sounds extremely lame in an administration which in its final four years emitted only public relations efforts on domestic policy.

In short, Nixon was not a pragmatist. He was an idealist, of sorts, at least a negative idealist. He set himself up as a good man amid a world full of enemies, and if his enemies would ultimately use the law against him, then the law was his enemy, too.

THE ATTORNEY GENERAL AND JUSTICE

John Mitchell

It was John Mitchell who, in the early days of Nixon's presidency, told civil rights activists, "Don't watch what we say, watch what we do."[31]

Like Nixon's similar remark, his statement is, in our minds, not a convincing argument that Nixon and his lawyers were pragmatists. Mitchell talked a tough line on new leftists and anti-war activists and followed up by zealously prosecuting a number of activists on conspiracy charges. All three of his most publicized cases (the Harrisburg 7, the Chicago 7, and Daniel Ellsberg) were marred by blunders.

Mitchell not only did what he said he would do, but he did it poorly. That kind of behavior is more the mark of a man whose vision is clouded by idealism than of a man who was a pragmatist.

Mitchell, who earned a reputation as a tough-minded law enforcement official because of his tough-talk and his masterminding of the Southern Strategy that won the 1968 election for Nixon, is emerging from the Watergate perjury trials as something between a crook and a bumbling fool.

Mitchell approved the $450,000 surveillance plan of G. Gordon Liddy which involved the burglarizing of National Democratic Headquarters, according to Jeb Stuart Magruder.

Mitchell denies the allegation, but it is barely conceivable that Mitchell who was the head of the Committee to Reelect the President, at the time would not have known about the plan.

And if he did, it would have been his duty, simply as a lawyer, let alone as Attorney General of the United States to, at a minimum, advise Liddy that his plan was in violation of the law.[32]

It is clear now that Mitchell, and any other Attorney General who would do so, violated the Code simply by remaining as Attorney General while heading the reelection campaign. It would be, at a minimum, the appearance of impropriety to hold employment representing the United States before the judicial system while at the same time running the campaign for a political candidate, regardless of whether that candidate is the President of the United States.[33]

That move alone would indicate that Mitchell was motivated more by loyalty to Richard M. Nixon than to effective representation of the United States, except in the sense that Mitchell and other men surrounding Nixon equated their service to the Richard M. Nixon presidency with service to the United States.

Regardless of his guilt or innocence regarding the conspiracy and obstruction of justice charges, John Mitchell's mistake originated in forgetting that his client was the United States, not Richard M. Nixon, and by attempting to serve two masters, or at least interpreting the two as one, he engaged in a conflict of interest.

John Mitchell was a lawyer for a cause, Richard M. Nixon. He should have been a lawyer for a client, the United States.

Richard Kleindeinst

Whereas John Mitchell had no difficulties knowing his loyalty was to Richard M. Nixon, his successor, Richard Kleindeinst, who was also a personal friend of Nixon's, at least saw a conflict between his loyalty to Nixon and his role as Attorney General.

Shortly after the burglary, Kleindeinst, then Attorney General, was approached by G. Gordon Liddy on a golf course and asked to free one of the burglars - McCord. Kleindeinst refused to become embroiled in the immediate coverup and immediately placed a call to Henry Petersen and told him not to give preferential treatment to any of the burglars. [34]

Kleindeinst, unfortunately, should have done more according to the Code, assuming Liddy's action was a clear indication that a coverup was underway and that Liddy was involved. (See Code). [35]

It could also be argued, and has been, that Kleindeinst committed a "misprison of a felony" by not immediately reporting Liddy's conversation with him to the appropriate authorities, in this case, his immediate subordinates, and especially Assistant Attorney General Henry Petersen. [36]

When Kleindeinst pled guilty to a midemeanor charge for failing to report to the Senate Judiciary Committee that Nixon had ordered him not to appeal a court decision favoring International Telegraph and Telephone Co., editorials appeared lamenting such leniency, especially considering the fact that Judge George Hart praised Kleindeinst as a man of the "highest integrity."[37]

We might dispute the "highest integrity" assessment, but Kleindeinst, unlike other Nixon friends and attorneys, did have a sense of legal ethics that might have been adequate in a pre-Watergate age.

Kleindeinst appears to have had a minimalist sense of legal ethics. He did refuse to cooperate with Liddy and he did instruct his subordinates not to free McCord. Later, on April 15, 1973, when Nixon hinted that Kleindeinst might prevent Justice Department action against Haldeman and Erlichman, Kleindeinst avoided directly answering the President. In the same conversation, he tells the President that it would be improper for him to be in contact with Haldeman, Erlichman, Mitchell, LaRue, and Mardian, since all were under investigation at the time.

Had Kleindeinst had a broader sense of ethics, he might also have avoided what he thought at the time was a private conversation with the President. Such a decision would have been based on the possibility that the President might be involved and that the President might indeed relay sections of this private conversation to those under investigation. The conversation did have the "appearance of impropriety" though in Kleindeinst's consideration, it might not have been so at the time.[38]

Kleindeinst might also have reacted more actively to Nixon's possibly improper question: "Why don't you do something about it?"[39]

According to the minimalist interpretation it would have been enough to do as Kleindeinst did and indirectly refuse to answer the question.

However, the import of criticism that Kleindeinst should have reported such indications of a coverup to his subordinates is that a more positive and active action is required, namely (see Code) that a lawyer should be both "zealous" on behalf of his client and that he is required to report violations of the law, or apparent violations of the law by brother attorneys to the relevant authorities.[40]

On the first point, Kleindeinst certainly came up short as a zealous prosecutor. His ethic did seem to incline him more to "not doing" something unethical than it did to simply doing his job as a prosecutor, particularly the chief prosecutor for the United States.

Whatever one thinks of Nixon, Kleindeinst's moral dilemma probably epitomizes the dilemma of every lawyer whose legal duty conflicts with his sense of moral responsibility. In Kleindeinst's case, his moral responsibility was the loyalty to a personal friend, Richard M. Nixon. And Kleindeinst apparently tried to solve the dilemma by neither aggressively pursuing legal roads that would have led to Nixon and at the same time, he did try to avoid breaking the law.

The obvious implication is that Kleindeinst would have emerged with a better reputation had he pursued his employment without regard to the effects of his legal action on what he considered his moral responsibility. The press and public apparently demanded this with what is unduly harsh criticism, though Kleindeinst was treated better by the legal profession by not being disbarred.

By disqualifying himself from aggressive action against the President and his men, Kleindeinst probably was in error, violating the spirit of the canons on zealous and competent representation of clients. He should have disqualified himself early in the game from the position of Attorney General, although he did sense the need for a Special Prosecutor for the same reasons.

Kleindeinst clearly appears to have violated the disciplinary rule of the new Code under Canon 1, which states that "A Lawyer possessing unprivileged knowledge of a violation .... shall report such knowledge to a tribunal or other authority empowered to investigate or act upon such violation."[41] This particular section of the Code is related in kind to the "misprison of a felony" and Kleindeinst's misdemeanor conviction.

Though this section of the new Code has been severely criticized within the profession for smacking of Gestapo tactics and for causing unreasonable conflicts with the principles of confidentiality, Kleindeinst's case seems set apart from this. As Attorney General, he clearly should have been concerned even with apparent violations of the law, especially by brother attorneys. Without pressing, he could simply have informed the investigators of his own department of both the Liddy and the Nixon conversations.

Thus, even though Kleindeinst did act upon a set of personal ethics, as a lawyer, he like Mitchell and Nixon paid the price for having a sense of duty other than to the law and the zealous representation of his client.

Henry Petersen

Perhaps the most interesting case of all the lawyers involved in Watergate is that of Henry Petersen, Assistant Attorney General, and the man originally in charge of prosecuting Watergate offenders.

As a civil servant, Petersen might have been expected to have the earmarks of a dedicated lawyer-for-hire, a man who at least knew his client was the United States and who would know the meaning of the term, "United States."

Petersen did, in fact, emerge with that image for the most part, and he accomplished that feat by giving an emotional speech to the Senate Watergate Committee in which he sounded "like a hard-nosed prosecutor who liked to nail hoods and put them in the slammer."[42]

The Washington Monthly makes a very good case that Petersen's television appearance, either through conscious fraud or blind stupidity was not an act.[43]

Included in the article is a laundry list of actions by Petersen, which when isolated seem very close to a list of overt acts in a conspiracy to obstruct justive indictment.

- Passed a message through John Dean, after failing to make phone contact, to John Mitchell that the grand jury "simply wanted to see if Mitchell told the same story as (Jeb) Magruder did."
- Reported to Dean that Magruder "got through (the grand jury) by the skin of his teeth."
- After receiving a telephone request from John Dean not to pursue a lead that connected Donald Segretti to Hunt, Petersen steered his assistant Silbert away from the investigation.
- Told the President, "I told Silbert, now, damn it Silbert, keep your eye on the mark. We are investigating Watergate; we are not investigating the whole

damn realm of politics, and I don't want you investigating the President's lawyer (Kalmbach)."

- Also told the President, "I've said to (U.S. Attorney Harold) Titus, 'We have to draw the line. We have no mandate to investigate the President. We investigate Watergate.'"

- Also told the President about Fred La-Rue's grand jury testimony which was damaging to Mitchell, and how Dean had further implicated Erlichman and others.[44]

In addition, Petersen committed innumerable sins of omission which indicated that he was less than a zealous prosecutor, mostly in the matter of not pursuing leads which led either to the President or to those close to him.[45]

Petersen's numerous meetings with Dean to recommend Petersen to the President "as the only man I know .... that really could tell us how this could be put together so that it did the maximum to carve it away with a minimum of damage to the individuals involved. He kept me informed .... He told me when we had problems .... he did make sure that the investigation was narrowed down to a very, very fine criminal thing which was a break for us."[46]

And Nixon himself made the classic boast to Haldeman and Erlichman that "I've got Petersen on a short leash."[47]

One cannot avoid making the invidious comparison that Petersen's sins of commission and omission were no different in kind than they would have been had he been investigating a Mafia crime and Nixon was the Don and Dean the consigliari.

Petersen made no bones about limiting the investigation to what he called "Watergate" - a term he used to describe the burglary only. He told the Senate Watergate Committee: "While I recognize that everybody is equal before the law, I also recognize that not everybody can be treated equally .... there are many, many concessions that are made because of office. I am conscious of the political consequences of my acts and I don't act like a blunderbuss."[48]

Petersen, quite clearly, epitomizes the lawyer who puts a cause before his client and adds a new dimension to my argument. The prosecutor cannot and should not consider the political implications of his actions. Political implications clearly fall into the category of personal bias and interpretations, which do not fall into the prosecutor's perview. Almost any action could be justified as "politically" unwise depending on the political opinion of the prosecutor.

Yet because chief prosecutors are chiefly appointed or elected through political mechanisms, this is a difficult ethic to enforce. Perhaps it can only be achieved through diligent enforcement by bar associations.

At any rate, the respect and esteem which Petersen earned before the Senate Watergate Committee for a television performance not in keeping with his performance in law is tragic.

WHITE HOUSE COUNSEL - DEAN

John Dean's role in the coverup is very well known, but there are two ethical implications that emerge from his actions. Dean's White

House career had two stages - the ethical and the unethical.

In the first stage, Dean was acting in the role of White House Counsel. Although the Attorney General has an advisory role to play for the President of the United States, he is chiefly the nation's top law enforcement officer, fulfilling a prosecutorial function. And the Attorney General represents the United States, the sovereign composed of the three branches of government.

In contrast, the White House Counsel is chiefly an advisor and represents only the White House, or the President, a segment of the Executive Branch. It would be the White House Counsel's job, more than the Attorney General's, to advise the President of the legal implications of his ordinary decisions and policies.

Section 3 under ethical considerations of Canon 7 states that "a lawyer serving as an advisor primarily assists his client in determining the course of future conduct and relations."[49]

While it could be said that Dean did attempt to fulfill this role, with hindsight one could say, not entirely facetiously, that Dean should have been disbarred for sheer incompetence. Dean's misplaced optimism was not dissimilar to Herbert Hoover's invocation that prosperity was just around the corner.

Section 5 of the Canon asserts that "A lawyer as advisor furthers the interest of his client by giving his professional opinion as to what he believes would likely be the ultimate decision of the courts on the matter at hand and by informing his client of the practical effect of such a decision."[50]

As a practical matter, when Henry Petersen was running the Justice Department investigation, Dean did have very good information about what was happening in the legal arena. But here his method, while zealous, certainly had the appearance of impropriety and as it later turned out, was an obstruction of justice and not within the bounds of the law.

In the same section the ethical consideration is: "He (the lawyer) may continue in the presentations of his client even though his client has elected to pursue a course of conduct contrary to the advice of the lawyer so long as he does not therby knowingly assist the client to engage in illegal conduct or to take a frivolous legal position."[51]

Clearly in the case of the hush money, the President was not pursuing an ethical course of conduct. Frequent mention is made of "black-mail" and Dean helped implement the payments.

Dean apparently never advised the President to make the choice that other presidents made when caught in similar scandals - to clean house, a painful but effective way to restore legal order, and under Dean's advice and without objection until later, the White House became more involved in an intricate coverup.

In the same section, "A lawyer should never encourage or aid his client to commit criminal acts or counsel his client on how to violate the law and avoid punishment therefore."[52]

Both the hush money discussions and Dean's consistent downplaying of queries to the "hang-out road" violated those considerations.

Dean waffled frequently on legal considerations. On March 21, 1973, he made several attempts to inform the President that certain proposed actions were illegal. He tells the President that his personal attorney has raised money and funneled it through the Cuban Committee to pay for the legal expenses of the Watergate burglars. The President says the cover is a good idea, but Dean notes that Haldeman, Erlichman, Mitchell, and himself are involved and "that is an obstructions of justice." Later he compares the money-raising operation to something the "Mafia people can do." He says it would be hard to do, but later suggests that Mitchell be charged with the operations. Later Dean explains how to "wash" the money.[53]

Dean was bothered by ethical considerations at least. He was obviously intelligent, but his error was probably in loyalty to the President and in lending the office too much awe. As a counsel, he frequently made decisions on a political and public relations basis rather than a legal basis.

In terms of the office of White House Counsel, or other counsels acting in advisory roles as lawyers, the implication is that such attorneys should confine their advice to legal considerations and avoid counsel based on economic, political, or social motivations. Certainly in the White House there were political, economic and public relations advisors. Dean's role should have been more specific to him. Organizations need a clearly defined opinion, unencumbered by other considerations. Legal advice given encumbered by other considerations will necessarily be biased. In this sense, compared to a lawyer acting in a advocacy role, the advisory counsel is a conservative influence. He states the legal case of a specific action, or may present a number of specific actions on his own and state their legal implications, or a number of legal remedies. But the actual drawing together of the social, political, economic, and legal implications is the task of the executive, not of the counsel.

Eventually Dean did begin cooperating with prosecutors, thus acting upon the ethical consideration to report violations of the law by brother attorneys and to report violations of the law according to the federal code.

The professional code section relating to reporting violations of the law by brother attorneys is especially sensitive to lawyers. And it is at least interesting that while Dean recovered some measure of respect from the public for his disclosures, he appears to have not achieved the same recovery in the legal profession. Though Dean's cooperation blew the lid off the Watergate coverup and even though his disclosures were corroborated in the White House transcripts, Dean received a harsh sentence for the obstruction of justice, particularly since relative to current Watergate defendants Dean was, as he termed himself, "a small fish."[54]

Ironically, Petersen's reputation was enhanced by his action in the Watergate events. Dean, who should be an American hero for his later actions, is disbarred and a convicted criminal.

Dean was wrong. He did act illegally and unethically. But he shifted his course to an ethical action that took an extraordinary amount of courage, particularly since nothing in the White House was conducive to following an ethical course at any point in time.

PERSONAL ATTORNEY - KALMBACH

As the personal attorney for Richard M. Nixon, citizen, Herbert Kalmbach's career was graced by incompetence and a singular lack of either personal or legal ethics.

Time said Kalmbach had a "solid but unspectacular career as a real estate lawyer," before he began working for Nixon. In 1968, his firm had only two lawyers. By 1970 that number jumped to 14, and in 1973 to 24, and his firm began handling such clients as United Air Lines, Dart Industries, Inc., the Marriott Corporation, and MCA, Inc.[55]

In the beginning Kalmbach only did a variety of minor tasks for the President, but gradually moved on to bigger and better things, including the arrangement of the purchase of Nixon's home in San Clemente and the installation of thousands of dollars' worth of improvements on the property that were charged off to "security" and paid for by the federal government. His partner arranged the equally controversial transfer of Nixon papers, and the $482,000 tax deduction for the gift.

Kalmbach appeared to have almost no qualms about the way he raised money or to whom and how he dished it out, as long as he did it for the President.[56]

In 1970, well before Watergate, he created a secret committee in violation of the Federal Corrupt Practices Act and collected 4 million dollars which was funneled to congressional candidates even though the committee had no chairman, no treasurer, and failed to file reports as required by law. He also collected $100.00 from J. File Symington, Ambassador to Trinidad and

Tobago, in return for a pledge for a higher-ranking ambassadorial post. In May, 1974, he pled guilty to violations of a felony charge for the secret committee arrangement. He pled guilty on a misdemeanor charge for the ambassadorial deal, which was never fulfilled.[57]

In addition he was one of the bagmen who picked up campaign contributions from milk producers just before the Nixon administration raised price supports in 1971. He also paid Segretti $45,000 for use in the dirty tricks campaign and raised the funds for $220,000 worth of payoffs to Watergate defendants.[58]

Time notes that Kalmbach was "above all else, an unswerving and unquestioning loyalist."[59]

Whatever he was, it is difficult to call Kalmbach a lawyer. He knew enough about law to cheat and circumvent the law at times, but in the end he wasn't even very good at that.

The prosecutors arranged relatively light charges for Kalmbach in return for cooperation at subsequent trials. One wonders what justice there was in arranging a light sentence for Kalmbach and a stiff sentence for Dean.

PERSONAL LAWYER - ST. CLAIR

Not all of the lawyers associated with Nixon were irresponsible and dishonest. James St. Clair, hired to represent Nixon as special counsel for Watergate-related offenses, was described by author George Higgins as a "hired gun."[60]

St. Clair epitomizes the lawyer who is willing to take almost any kind of case and has himself said "every person is entitled to be represented by the lawyer of his choice."[61]

St. Clair defended William Sloane Coffin Jr. against a charge of conspiracy to encourage draft evasion and later represented a Boston school committee challenging mandatory desegregation of its schools.[62]

That kind of eye for law and disregard for personal philosophy prompted Coffin to note that "The trouble with St. Clair is that he is all case and no cause."[63]

St. Clair is generally described as a cunning courtroom lawyer, but he is also known for excellent research.[64]

With a ridiculously weak case, previously covered in the section on Nixon, St. Clair did a remarkable job of representing Nixon. His only available tools were delays, particularly as a tactic for wearing down public opinion against the President and seeing Nixon past an impeachment threat. Harvard's Law School's Alan Derchowitz noted that, "If Nixon is innocent, has nothing to hide, the St. Clair is doing a terrible job because he is making it appear as though Nixon has something to hide. If he is guilty, then St. Clair is doing a great job."[65]

Law professor John Flynn argued that St. Clair's tactic of delay was a disservice to the nation. The University of Chicago's Harry Kalvin Jr. made a similar argument.[66]

While it is true that the delays may have harmed the country and weakened it leadership, St. Clair would have been violating his professional responsibility had he not resorted to what was, in his opinion, the best representation for his client.

St. Clair might have privately argued that Nixon should resign or seek a quick decision for "the good of the country," but if his client was committed to extricating himself, then it was St. Clair's duty to present him with the best possible defense without regard to the consequences against the public interest.

For with the public vindictiveness against Nixon, there was every danger that Nixon could have been run out of office with improper impeachment procedures, inadequate defenses before the court of law that might have left facts uncovered but the defendants convicted, and it could well be argued that such defenses might have severe implications both on the political process and the legal tradition of "innocent until proven guilty."

St. Clair's Supreme Court arguments were legally specious, but a President had acted upon those arguments of absolute executive privilege, and had St. Clair not made every attempt to uphold those arguments the Supreme Court would never have been able to form satisfactory arguments against them; a consequence which might have led to a presidency in future generations which would act even more upon principles of absolute power and exemption from the laws of the land than Nixon had.

By acting solely in the interest of his client, without regard to personal bias or a sense of personal moral responsibility except to the law and his client, St. Clair served a greater public service than a lawyer who might have inadequately defended Nixon in the greater interest of the nation.

SPECIAL PROSECUTOR - JAWORSKI

Although the Special Prosecutor's office was technically a branch of the Justice Department, it was, in effect, an independent agent because of the Justice Department's regulations requiring that Jaworski could not be fired without the concensus of congressional leaders.

Leon Jaworski, though far less flashy, is in many ways similar to St. Clair.

A conservative Texas Democrat who had supported Nixon in 1972, Jaworski seemed an unlikely prosecutor of Watergate-related crimes. Like St. Clair, Jaworski was also a maverick. In conservative Texas, he once defended a liberal school board which was under attack from conservatives, and prosecuted former Mississippi Governor Ross Barnett on criminal contempt charges for trying to block desegregation.[67]

Unlike St. Clair, Jaworski seemed much more directly concerned with ethical principles and maintaining his own professional integrity. In fact he was scrupulous in that matter. On principle, he refused to meet with Nixon, and refused invitations to see him. When St. Clair challenged Dean's credibility as a witness out of court, Jaworski icily accused St. Clair of unprofessional conduct.

Jaworski had another characteristic which was fortunate for the times. He has a distaste for publicity, and was primarily given more to tenacious legal research than courtroom dramatics. Considering the political delicacy of the case, it was paramount that the legal case against Watergate offenders be technically sound and avoid any appearance of partisanship or personal vindictiveness.

Though Jaworski had a distinctly different style than St. Clair, they had a common emphasis on the law and a sense of what their legal duty was. Neither was given to personal bias. Neither was dedicated to a "cause" other than zealous representation of their "case" in the best possible legal light.

CONCLUSION

There is a constant dilemma in the legal profession. Laws are inflexible and cannot be changed except by men, and when they do change, the change always lags behind the moral sensibilities of men. Moreover, laws are written in stone and apply to entire group of men. So a dilemma arises when laws do not seem adequate to meet the needs of men, and sometimes seems to hold back the progress of peoples.

Lawyers can perceive the inadequacy of laws and the injustice of our system of justice perhaps better than laymen, and there is a great temptation for men of conscience to feel that someimes it is necessary to operate outside of, or beyond, the law, for the law is an inefficient and slow system of accomplishing social goals.

It is easily possible to argue that social change can best take place by methods other than the law.

But the law is still the foundation upon which society is built, and it is the task of lawyers to uphold the foundation and to improve it according to the changing needs of men. Someone has to preserve this foundation. And those who are dedicated to preserving the law are lawyers.

If a lawyer, acting in a capacity as a lawyer, puts as his first priority something other than preserving the integrity of our legal system, whether that "other" is a moral principle, a cause, a movement, or a man, then that foundation is severely threatened. There is every temptation to circumvent the law, to mold it according to one's own personal vision, and that operation necessarily perverts the adversary system and it perverts the law. It is destructive.

I have tried to show that those lawyers who were most destructive of the ends of society were those who, while acting in their capacity as lawyers, tried to achieve those ends directly, by going outside the law.

And those lawyers who served society best were those who did not think of the public interest first, but those who thought of their client and their duty to the courts first.

It has been suggested that the men who created Watergate were converted away from "law and order" by the radicals of the 1960's, people who sought to improve society by going outside of the law, people who sought to improve society by violating the law.

On February 28, 1973, Nixon said to John Dean:

> Don't you try to disrupt their meetings? Didn't they try to disrupt ours? (Expletive deleted) They threw rocks, ran demonstrations, shouted, cut the sound system, and let the tear gas in at night.[68]

In the end, there was no difference between Nixon, Mitchell, Kleindeinst, Petersen, Dean, and Kalmbach, and those who threw rocks, and ran demonstrations. Perhaps Nixon and his attorneys committed the greater crime. They were lawyers.

THIS IS A REPRINT FROM *ISSUES IN THE LAW OF CRIMINAL CORRECTIONS*. VOL. 1. PILGRIMAGE PRESS, (1979).

[1] Cheap and sleazy were frequent adjectives in newspaper editorials following the release of the transcripts.

[2] *Time*, May 13, 1974, p. 13.

[3] Ibid.

[4] A phrase used disparangingly to describe St. Clair. See *Time*, March 25, 1974, p. 13.

[5] *American Bar Association Code of Professional Responsibility*, Canon 7.

[6] Weckstein, Donald C., "Training for Professionalism," 4 *Coun. L. Rev.* 409, 1971-72.

[7] Perhaps not since the famous statement, "You won't have Nixon to kick around," after the 1962 California gubenatorial election. Although it was not uncommon for Presidents to refer to themselves as "presidents" during public speeches, Nixon seemed to prefer referring to himself as "the President" even in private conversations. See *White House Transcripts*, Appendix 48, April 27, 1973, p. 777-804.

[8] *The White House Transcripts*, Appendix 1, September 15, 1972, p. 57-69; *Time*, May 13, 1974, p. 20.

[9] Ibid.

[10] Ibid.

[11] *Time*, July 22, 1974, p. 19.

[12] "The Illustrated Secret History of Watergate, Part II," *New York Magazine*, June 24, 1974, p. 50.

[13] Ibid.

[14] "The Illustrated Secret History of Watergate, Part I," *New York Magazine*, June 27, 1974, p. 51.

[15] Ibid.

[16] St. Clair argued that he was not actually engaged in defending Richard Nixon but in representing the Office of the Presidency. See *Time*, March 25, 1974, p. 14.

[*17*] 94 S. Ct. 3090 (1974).

[18] Supra, note 17, p. 3095.

[19] Supra, note 17, p. 3100.

[20] *Time*, July 22, 1974, p. 12.

[21] Supra, note 17, p. 3100.

[22] Supra, note 17, p. 3100-3102.

[23] Supra, note 17, p. 3101-3102.

[24] Supra, note 17, p. 3100-3102.

[25] Supra, note 17, p. 3105-3107.

[26] *Time*, May 22, 1974, p. 30.

[27] Supra, note 17, p. 3107.

[28] Supra, note 17, p. 3107.

[29] Supra, note 13, p. 49-50.

[30] *Time*, May 13, 1974, p. 30.

[31] Supra, note 12, p. 49.

[32] Supra, note 14, p. 53.

[33] Supra, note 5, Canon 9.

[34] Levine, Arthur, "The Man Who Nailed Gordon Liddy," *The Washington Monthly*, December, 1974, p. 29-30.

[35] Supra, note 5, Canon 9.

[36] Supra, note 34, p. 46.

[37] Supra, note 34, p. 46.

[38] *The White House Transcripts*, Appendix 23, April 15, 1973, p. 476-485; *Time*, May 13, 1974.

[39] Ibid.

[40] Supra, note 5, Canon 7.

[41] Supra, note 5, Canon 1.

[42] Supra, note 34, p. 48.

[43] Ibid.

[44] Supra, note 34, p. 38-48.

[45] Ibid.

[46] Ibid.

[47] Ibid.

[48] Ibid.

[49] Supra, note 5, Canon 7.

[50] Ibid.

[51] Ibid.

[52] Ibid.

[53] *The White House Transcripts*. Appendix 6 and 7, March 21, 1973, p. 132-194.

[54] *Time*, March 13, 1974, p. 19.

[55] *Time*, March 13, 1974, p. 28.

[56] Ibid.

[57] Ibid.

[58] Ibid.

[59] Ibid.

[60] *Time*, March 25, 1974, p. 12-17.

[61] Ibid.

[62] Ibid.

[63] Ibid.

[64] Ibid.

[65] Supra, note 60, p. 17.

[66] Ibid.

[67] Supra, note 55, p. 13.

[68] *The White House Transcripts*, Appendix 2, February 28, 1973, p. 69-93.

CONTEMPORARY ISSUES AND TRENDS
IN COURT REFORM

When the writers of the Constitution penned their manuscript, they envisioned the courts to, "play an important but limited role in protecting private property and defending liberties against leglislative encroachment."[1] Today, however, the court systems in the United States have been given the elusive mandate of administering justice. The courts are to carry out this mandate amidst conflicting political and social pressures. Frequently, this is to be done with insufficient resources. In a recent address to New York University, Chief Justice Warren E. Burger stated that, "state and federal court systems could break down before the end of the century because of the burden of work being placed on them."[2] Concerned with the task of seeing justice effectively and equitably administered, court reformers are not appeased by fatalistic predictions as those stated by Chief Justice Burger, but rather pursue the enactment of reforms in our court systems. My analysis will be directed at some of the pertinent current issues and trends supported by court reformers today.

For a thorough understanding of court reform efforts today, it is necessary to trace the history of court reforms. The most noteworthy scholar heralding the cry for court reform in the early part of this century was Roscoe Pound, who became the Dean of the Harvard Law School. In 1906, he made a plea to the American Bar Association about what he viewed to be the three

archaic features of the American judicial
system. These three were: first, that there
existed a multiplicity of the courts causing du-
plication, waste and inefficiency; second, that
concurrent jurisdiction is out of place in a
modern society; and third, that jurisdictional
boundaries and unequal workloads lead to much
waste of judicial power.[3] Pound's plea brought
about an American Bar Association Committee designed to propose reform legislation for the judiciary.

In a continued response to this plea for reform, in 1913 the American Judiciary Society was
established to promote the efficient administration of justice.[4] This movement concerned with
court administration continued to spread to the
states. In 1913 Wisconsin created a judicial
council. In 1923 Massachusetts and Ohio followed suit. By 1949 similar councils were established in 37 of the then existing 49
states.[5]

A spokesman for reform in the federal courts
came in the person of former President Taft. He
praised the simple and flexible procedures of
the British system and admonished America to
learn from the English example. Taft gave six
explicit recommendations to Congress for improving the American court system. They were:

"1) Abolish the antiquated system which
separates law and equity;
2) Place the rules of procedure completely under the control of the Supreme
Court or a council of judges;
3) Reduce costs to a minimum, with as
much as possible borne by the government
rather than by litigants;

4) Confer upon the head of the federal judicial system the authority to redistribute judges to help eliminate backlogs;

5) Reduce the number of cases the Supreme Court is required to review; and

6) Pass a federal workman's compensation act."[6]

Most of these were enacted into law in the following years.[7]

The third major figure in the history of court reform emerging in the 1930's was Arthur T. Vanderbilt. While president of the American Bar Association he emphasized the need to reform state courts. Some of the issues he brought to the forefront were: improving pretrial procedure, methods of selecting juries, improving trial practice, improving the law of evidence, simplifying appellate procedure, controlling state adminstrative agencies, and improving judicial organization and administration.[8]

During the war years of the 1940's reform efforts were set aside. However, the movement was revitalized during the 1950's. The Institute of Judicial Administration was founded in 1952 under the guidance of Arthur Vanderbilt. The institute is closely related to the New York University School of Law and has a staff that conducts research on state court systems. Another effort towards court reform in the 1950's was the Conference on Court Congestion and Delay for reviewing court management problems organized by Attorney General Herbert Brownell.[9]

One of the significant events that occurred in the decade of the sixties was the release of the President's task force report on the courts in 1967.[10] Although the report offered numerous recommendations, its major thrust supported the adoption of unified state court systems along the lines of those recommended by the American Bar Association, the National Municipal League, and the American Judicature Society. It has been said that, "It was this report, perhaps more than any other, that served as the impetus for states to revise and reform what can only be termed as an extremely outdated and archaic judicial system."[11]

Historically, Roscoe Pound has been considered to be the father, and William Howard Taft and Arthur T. Vanderbilt the sons, of court reform in the United States. Under the impetus of their ideas and efforts numerous reform efforts have been attempted to increase the efficiency and effectiveness of both our federal and state court systems. Among the varied efforts currently supported by reformers are court unificiation, merit selection of the judiciary, and increased use of technology in the courts. On that basis I will address the following three issues: 1) Is court unification a viable alternative to the decentralized systems that exist in many states?[12] 2) Is merit selection of the judiciary preferable over other measures of judicial selection?, and 3) Will the increased use of modern technology offer beneficial alternatives for increased court efficiency?

Issue #1, Is Court Unification a Viable Alternative to the Decentralized Systems that Exist in Many States?

The first directives for court unification were espoused by Roscoe Pound in his address to

the American Bar Association in 1906. He later
stated in his article, "Principles and Outline
of a Modern Unified Court System," that

> Unification of the courts would go far to
> enable the judiciary to do adequately
> much which is desperation of efficient
> legal disposition by fettered courts,
> tied to cumbersome and technical proce-
> dure, we have been committing more and
> more to administrative boards and commis-
> sions.[13]

The American Bar Association responded to
Pound's proposals for reform. The resolutions
the Association established came to be known as
the Parker-Vanderbilt Standards.[14] Included
among the standards was the recommendation for a
simplified court system. The ABA later adopted
nearly all of the proposals of Pound and his
successors in its *Standards Relating to Court
Organization*. Another early model for the unification of state court systems that was created
in response to Pound's proposals was published
by the American Judicature Society in 1920. It
had been drafted at the request of the National
Municipal League.[15] These early models laid
the foundation for the efforts in unification
that have been instituted in recent years.

Although there is some disagreement among
proponents of unification, a review of the literature reveals that there are five feature on
which there is nearly universal agreement.
These five features are: consolidation and simplification of the court structure, centralized
rule-making, centralized management, centralized
budgeting, and state financing. G. Allen Tarr

states that, "(u)nderlying these specific reforms is a broad indictment of non-unified court systems."[16] Proponents of unification feel that non-unified systems cannot achieve equity and efficiency because in essence they are non-systems. In these non-systems, the uniform administration of justice is hindered by fragmentation and complexity; and, the lack of accountability in the decentralized approach makes management and planning difficult. With that in mind, unification is viewed as offering viable solutions to the courts. This author will examine the five features of unification as explained by their proponents.[17]

The first feature as listed is the consolidation and simplification of the court structure. As Larry Berkson phrases it, this feature is, "at the heart of court unification." Court consolidation is the simplification of court structures by giving the same jurisdiction at each level of the system and establishing clear jurisdictional boundaries between levels.[18] Vanderbilt stresses that his simplification of the courts that would replace the complicated judicial structures that exist in many jurisdictions is, "fundamental to the administration of justice."[19] Although there is wide agreement that the courts should be consolidated, there is disagreement over how many tiers should be in the remaining system. One of the major disputes is whether there should be a two-tier or single-tier trial court. During the 1960's the American Bar Association, the President's Commission on Law Enforcement and the Administration of Justice, and in 1971 the Advisory Commission on Intergovernmental Relations expressed their support of the two-tier model. In years following, the American Bar Association switched its support to the single-tier model. The National Conference on the Judiciary and the National Advisory Commission on Criminal Justice Standards and Goals also voiced support for the single-tier model. The National Municipal League has fluctuated in its support between the two models.[20] Supporting the more popular position of late, Allan Ashman and Jeffrey Parness state,

> "One state-wide court of general jurisdiction probably is all that is required within a unified court system. However, under certain circumstances, a state-wide limited jurisdiction court might function quite well and differ little from division of a single state-wide trial court of general jurisdiction which handles only minor matters. Consequently, it is possible for a system with two, three or even four levels of courts to be characterized as having a simplified court structure. The key lies not in the number of courts handling cases but in the state's method for handling cases brought before its courts.[21]

The second dispute about consolidation is whether or not there should be an intermediate court of appeals. Roscoe Pound clearly felt such a court was unnecessary. The American Judicature Society has concurred with Pound. Even so, there has been broad support for this as seen in the recommendations of the American Bar Association's Model Judicial Article of 1962, the National Municipal League's Model State Constitution of 1963, the American Bar Association's Standards of 1974, and the Minnesota Judicial Council Report of 1974.[22]

Although there are varied opinions as to what is the most desirable organizational structure for the consolidated court system (see Appendix A for some examples) there is a concensus that some form of consolidation is advantageous for the court. There are three identifiable benefits from such an approach. One benefit is that backlogs could be reduced by the flexible assignment of judges in the large trial courts. A second benefit would be more efficient use of facilities and equipment through the elimination of duplicative purchases, and the consolidation of duplicative support services. This point was substatiated through a study conducted on the consolidation of the courts in the city of Athens and Clarke County, Georgia. Four per cent of the total budget, which in this case amounted to $5440, was saved through more efficient use of facilities and equipment.[23] Thirdly, it is thought that consolidation can improve the court's capacity to do justice. Two factors contributing to the increased capacity for justice are: 1) more qualified judges should be recruited since there will be no one exclusively assigned to lower court duties, and 2) the standardization of rules and procedures should eliminate litigants initiating cases in the wrong courts.[24]

The second feature characterizing unification of courts is centralized rulemaking. Prior to 1848 the courts controlled their own procedure. However, in that year a Field Code was adopted in New York dividing the responsibilities for judicial administration between the legislature and the judiciary. This model began to be copied by other states. By the turn of the century alternatives were being proposed by reformers. In 1917 in the second draft of the Statewide Judicature Society proposed that most rulemaking authority be granted to a judical council. In 1938 the American Bar Association, joined by Roscoe Pound in 1940, viewed that rulemaking powers should be given back to the judiciary. In 1942 the National Municipal League took the position that the legislature should have some voice in the matter. The position universally adhered to today is that rulemaking authority should be vested exclusively in the Supreme Court.[25]

Reformers cite three reasons why the state Supreme Court should be granted all of the rulemaking authority. One is that the Supreme Court has more interest in the improvement of the judiciary than any other body and consequently is more responsive to the need for change. A second reason is that its knowledge and expertise of court operations will enhance the effectiveness of its rules. Thirdly, it is hoped that rulemaking by the Supreme Court will not be as susceptible to partison considerations as other ruling bodies might be.[26]

The third feature of court unification is centralized management. This involves centralized accountability and authority by creating a hierarchal structure giving primary administrative responsibility to the state chief justice and to his court administrator.[27] Roscoe Pound was an early proponent of giving the chief justice this authority. Advocating such a measure, he states:

> "Supervision of the judicial-business administration of the whole court should be committed to the chief justice .... He

should have authority to make reassignments or temporary assignments of judges to particular branches or divisions or localities according to the amount of work to be done, and the judges at hand to do it."[28]

Every major study since 1942 has, along with Pound, taken the position that administrative responsibilities for the court system should be granted to the chief justice. In addition, most of these studies also call for a court administrator to assist the chief justice in these duties.[29] The National Advisory Commission on Criminal Justice Goals and Standards goes a step further in recommending that the state court administrator appoint local court administrators. This is to enable the policies made at the top of the hierarchy to be uniformly applied throughout the system, thereby providing coordination, accountability, and continuity.[30] The American Bar Association takes a different position. The Association adheres to the view that the presiding judge should appoint the trial court executive. The question of appointment of administrators remains unresolved. In either case, the essential feature here is the handling of administrative responsibilities.[31]

The actual responsibilities that the chief justice will supervise are: the assignment of judges and cases, the qualifications, hiring and firing of personnel, space and equipment, centralized record keeping and statistics gathering, centralized planning, financial administration, educational programs for court-related personnel, research for the state court system, and the dissemination of information about the operations of the state court system.[32]

Proponents of unification give four major reasons as to why it is advantageous to centralize the accountibility and authority for all of these responsibilities. One reason is that efficiency will be increased by the elimination of duplicative planning efforts at the local level. Secondly, the system-wide planning that will take place should encourage more efficient use of court resources. Thirdly, it provides for reassignments of both judges and support personnel to equalize the workloads. Finally, uniformity and equity are brought about by the centralized managment which governs procedures and directives throughout the system.[33]

The fourth feature of court unification is unitary budgeting. This places the responsibility of preparing and administering the budget for all operating expenses of the court system in the hands of the administrative head of the judiciary. This feature was not recommended by the early reformers, but, rather, it was first proposed in the American Bar Association's Model Judiciary Article of 1962. A year later the National Municipal League joined the ABA in support of unitary budgeting. Under this concept neither the executive nor the legislature has any say or power to veto.[34] Only twelve states have budgeting systems that closely resemble this model.[35]

There are four ways identified by proponents of unitary budgeting that it is to benefit court operations. One is simply that the cost of budget preparations are reduced through centralization. A second is that having specialized personnel prepare the budget, it will more accurately reflect court operations. A third way the court operations are benefitted is through the double check on the budget by having the local courts justify their expenditures to the state budgetary and in addition, the budgetary authority to the state legislature. Lastly, this method of budgeting,

> "promotes effective judicial management by facilitating the adoption of their administrative reforms and collating information about the courts' needs and expenditures."[36]

The fifth and final characteristic of court unification is state financing. This means that all local fines and fees should be transferred to the state and that the state should finance the entire judicial system. This along with unitary budgeting is a more recent addition to unification schemes. The first explicit proposal for state financing was made by the National Municipal League in 1963. Most commissions since that time have voiced support for state financing.[37] Two reasons for implementing state financing are stated in the literature. One reason is to ensure some degree of parity throughout court services. The second reason is to enhance integration of the state judicial system through planning and managment.[38]

In spite of the widespread support given for court unification, there are five criticisms that have heralded against it. The foremost criticism is that, "Administrative centralization is an overly simplistic solution to all court management ills."[39] Unification treats the court systems as if they existed in a vacuum. It does not take into account the dynamic interactions of the courts with political and social systems. The courts need to reflect the divisions, structures, and processes of these other systems to be effective in a dynamic society. Even though the highly centralized organizational structure proselytized by unification supporters may be appropriate for other governmental systems, it is criticized as inappropriate for the courts.[40] Geoffrey Gallas points out three reasons why. These are: the county-based nature of judicial and quasi-judicial functions, the professional status of most key figures in the judicial system, and the underdeveloped state of court administration.[41] These points made by Gallas lead to the next three criticisms of unification.

The next criticism to note is based on Gallas' view that judicial and quasi-judicial functions are county based in nature. Due to this factor, courts have been percieved to be local and should be responsive to local needs. As stated by Broder, Porter, and Smathers, "courts must strike a balance between providing equality of treatment under the law and meeting unique law enforcement needs of the communities they serve...."[42] Critics argue that court unification schemes diminish court's responsiveness to local values through their efforts to centralize and consolidate. In addition, this movement is seen as a threat to the close relationship that traditionally exists between local courts and local governments. The local flexibility in carrying out the functions of the court would be altered under unification.[43]

A third criticism relates to the professional status of judges and attorneys. Organizational theory suggests that professionals of this nature prefer operating with autonomy as opposed to being subjected to strict hierarchal structure. A free environment facilitates creativity, innovation, and expertise.[44] A move towards the hierarchy might be viewed as stifling to judges and attorneys who would rank as M4's on Chris Argyris' Immaturity-Maturity model.

A fourth criticism hurled at unification is that the "state of the art in court management is unsettled."[45] It is claimed that proponents of unification are in disagreement about the purposes and characteristcs of the reform effort. Until the concept is developed to maturity and a greater concensus is reached, it will be questioned and resisted by the critics.

The final criticism that will be noted here is related to the first. In an era of modern management thought, where contingency theory is widely taught and widely received, the appropriateness of applying classical theory to judicial systems is to be questioned. Reformers have overlooked the fact that the classical theory is outdated. Inroads are beginning to be made in applying contemporary management theory to court reform. Two of the forerunners in applying modern theory to the unification movement are David Saari and Geoffrey Gallas. It is their position that unificiation perpetrates overcentralization and rigidification of court operations.[46]

Even though there is much discussion in the literature about the perceived advantages or disadvantages of court unification, there exists little empirical evidence to support the views of its proponents or critics.[47] In addition, the research that does exist is,

> "complicated by reform goals which are
> stated in idealized ambiguous and non-op-
> erational terms and by assumptions that
> these desired but slippery outcomes (for
> examples, equity, accountability, better
> justice, efficiency or effectiveness)
> flow automatically from proposed rem-
> edies."[48]

Consequently, the advantages or disadvantages of
implementing court unification programs have yet
to be clearly established by researchers.

Even with the status of the research in a
tenuous position, projections for the future
trend of court unification are quite clear. The
projections in the literature favor the increased use of unification as a reform effort in
the courts. Allan Ashman and Jeffrey Parness
confirm this in their statement:

> "The concept will continue to play a cru-
> cial role in all attempts to reform the
> structure, organization, and administra-
> tion of the various American court sys-
> tems because the applications of the
> principles of court unification are es-
> sential to the achievement of efficient
> and just systems."[49]

However, those who acknowledge and support such
a trend, viewing unification as a viable alternative to existing court systems, emphasize that
unification *alone* will not be a panacea for all
of the existing problems in the courts.[50]

Issue #2, Is Merit Selection of the Judiciary Preferable Over Other Measures of Judicial Selection in the States?

Judges play a very meaningful role in the dispensing of justice in the criminal justice system.[51] Consequently, there is much concern about the process of selecting the judiciary. Even though, "(n)o selection system gaurantees high quality." nore does any one, "system uniformly select low quality" there is increasing discussion among scholars about the advantages of merit selection over other measures of selecting judges.[52] I will now examine the selecting systems that have been used in American and evaluated whether or not merit selection is a preferable model.

In the early days of this country judges were appointed by the King of England. Following the American Revolution, appointment of judges was continued in the thirteen colonies.[53] However, during the Jacksonian Revolution, election of judges began. Judges participated in political campaigning. The slogan of the day was "To the victor belongs the spoils."[54] By the time the Civil War started, 24 of the existing 34 states were electing their judiciary. As each new state was added, election of the judiciary was adopted. Even so, disenchantment with the elective approach began as early as 1853. By 1873 a movement to return to an appointive system was gaining support in New York. In that same year nonpartisan elections were used for the first time in Cook County Illinois.[55] Criticism of this option began almost immediately. In 1906, in his address to the American Bar Association, Roscoe Pound criticized all forms of judicial elections in his statement, "putting courts into politics, and compelling judges to become politicians in many jurisdictions .... almost destroyed the traditional respect for the bench."[56]

Disgruntled with the elective systems, reformers began to support the merit plan for selecting judges that was originated by Albert M. Kates, one of the founders of the American Judicature Society.[57] The plan was composed of the following three features:

> "--a judicial council composed of presiding judges would nominate candidates for judgeships;
> --the state's elected chief justice would actually choose judges; and
> --a judges' tenure would depend upon winning a noncompetitive election."[58]

The first time a version of this was instituted was in 1940 in the state of Missouri. This selection system which has come to be known as the Missouri Plan, has a nonpartisan nominating commission comprised of three attorneys selected by the Missour Bar Association, three lay persons selected by the governor, and the state supreme court chief justice. The governor selects the name of the judge to be appointed from a list of three names submitted by the nominating commission. After serving a one year probationary period the appointee runs unopposed on a nonpartisan judicial ballot for voter approval. If the judge wins a majority vote, he or she will serve a full term of office.[59]

Today, both partisan and nonpartisan elections as well as appointment systems are being used throughout the states. Partisan elections are used to select some of the judges in eight states and most or all of the judges in seventeen states. On the other hand a commission is used to aid the governor in thirty-one states. Out of these, twenty of the states use the panels for the initial selection of a judge, with the other eleven using them only to fill vacancies.[60]

Although, when elections systems for selecting judges were first implemented they were done so for the purpose of ensuring the popular sovereignty known as Jacksonian Democracy, their value has come under attack.[61] Larry Berkson, the director of educational programs at the American Judicature Society, has synthesized what he views to be the five major criticisms of electoral methods of selecting judges. The first criticism is that election systems do not do what they claim: provide a system in which people can rationally choose between candidates for an office. This is based on several factors. These factors are:

1) many judges are initially appointed to fill vacancies;
2) judges are elected infrequenetly due to long tenure;
3) incumbants succeed with little difficulty, and are often unopposed; and
4) where there are contests there is an absence of vital issues.[62]

The second criticism is that elective systems are based on the false argument that voters are attentive and well-informed. In actuality, voters base their decisions on appearance or personality.

The third criticism is that exceptionally well-qualified people have a distaste for politics and campaigning, therefore they choose not to get involved in elections. A fourth criticism is that the independent decision-making capacity is compromised when a judge obtains and maintains his or her office by responding to the views of the majority. It is the responsibility of judges to protect the rights of the minority and ensure equal protection under the Constitution. The final criticism that Berkson notes about election systems in general is that campaigning for reelection leads to both a neglect of official duties and potential for political favors and possibly illegal activity.[63]

In addition to these criticisms of election systems in general there are some criticisms that have been directed specifically at partison elections. One such criticism is that rather than top quality people being selected to run, selection comes as a reward for party support.[64]

This leads to the election of judges enmeshed in party politics and the manipulation of judgeships by political machines. In addition, as Vanderbilt pointed out, a judge elected under these conditions cannot be active in pursuing judicial reform because of his political ties.[65] Another criticism hailed at partisan elections is that it allows for the public to vote for a judge on the basis of his party affiliation rather than on his own merits.[66]

Nonpartisan elections have also been singled out for criticism. The American Judicial Society considers it to be the worst method available for judicial selection in America. They have found that use of nonpartisan selection is accompanied by a lack of concern for the experience, character, and ability of the candidate. Instead his or her financial backing, media exposure, and family name have greater weight.[67] Consequently, nonpartisan along with partisan elective systems are strongly criticized in the literature.

The last of the three approaches to be evaluated here is merit selection. The merit selection plan is given strong support by the President's Commission on Law Enforcement and Administration of Justice.[68] Even so, it remains a hotly debated topic. It is viewed by its supporters to be a means of overcoming the weaknesses identified with the election systems. The supporters point out that it has been widely approbated in areas that it has ben implemented. On reason is that it improves the caliber of judges. This is true to the experience of Missouri, and in other areas as well, according to the authorities Watson and Downing.[69] Even with its strong support, merit selection is not free from criticism.

The critics have a variety of objections to the merit plan. One objection is that there is not adequate representation of all segments of the community in the initial selection.[70] Another objection is that it is removing the selection from the hands of the electorate and giving the choice to the legal community.[71] A third objection is that politics are not removed from the process.[72] Although it is true that not *all* politics are removed, proponents defend this sytem by claiming that the main issue involved in the selection is not the removal of politics, but the selection of the most qualified individual. A fourth objection is that merit selection leads to life-tenured judgeships.[73] Proponents defend this by pointing out that this pehomenon may be attributed to the fact that competent judges are taking office and therefore the public supports them in retention elections. They also take note of the fact that the incumbant has an almost equal chance of life-tenure in popular elections. One last arguemnt made is that popular elections educate the public, but merit plans do not. Berkson points out two flaws to this argument. One is that judges in most popular elections run unopposed. The second is that when a contest exists the platforms are generally alike and are issueless. Consequently, the electoral system fails to educate the public as well.

There has been little effort to conduct objective empirical studies to substantiate the claims of either proponents or the critics of merit selection. Thus, there is only a modicum of facts on which to guide policy makers on this issue. However, the trends seem to be moving towards the increased adoption of merit selection. As Berkson evaluated its use he found that, "in the last decade, 28 states adopted or extended their commission plan," of merit selection which is consistent not only with national trends, but international trends as well.[74] This country's method of selecting judiciary has evolved from a system of appointment that was subject to abuses by the authority exercising this power, to a system of election that has been subject to a variety of political abuses, and is now moving towards a system where judges are selected on their merits by nonpartisan nominating commissions.

Issue #3, Will the Increased Use of Modern Technology Offer Beneficial Alternative For Increased Court Efficiency?

On August 10, 1970 Chief Justice Warren E. Burger addressed the American Bar Association on the subject of court reform. As he was urging for changes to be made he made the statement:

> "Efficiency must never be the controlling test of criminal justice but the work of the courts can be efficient without jeopardizing basic safeguards. Indeed the delays in trials are often one of the gravest threats to individual rights. Both the accused and the public are entitled to a prompt trial."[75]

Some people advocate the use of videotaping by courts as one means of reducing delays and backlogs in courts, thereby increasing efficiency and safeguarding individual rights. Sherwood Allen Salvan, a New York attorney, is one such person. He thinks that the legal profession has failed to utilize the modern technology available to it. This has led to four detrimental consequences.

> "(1) a continuing drain on the limited resources of time and energy available to lawyers,
> (2) a severe taxing of the court administration systems, with a consequent overcrowding of court calendars,
> (3) higher costs for all parties concerned, and half the numbers here too rights.[76]

This portion of my discussion will be directed towards how the courts can be reformed through the increased use of modern technology. Specifically to be examined are: videotaped depositions, videotaped trials, and videotaping for appeals.

Videotape was invented in 1956 by the Ampex Corporation. It was used for the first time on November 30th of that year on a CBS news broadcast. The first documented use of videotape in a court was December, 1971. At that time a deposition of a physician was taken for the personal injury case of *McCall v. Clemens*. Its most extensive use has been in Ohio by Judge James J. McCrystal. Judge McCrystal has conducted entire trials, except for the voir dires and opening and closing arguments on videotapes.[77]

Videotapes have had their widest use and warmest reception by the courts for the purpose of taking depositions. When it was instituted in Ohio the only requirement was that the side of the case taking the deposition inform the opponent that it would be used.[78] Consequently, its use was quickly promoted. Subsequently thousands of deposition have been taped. Videotaped depositions are useful for witnesses unavailable due to illness, advanced age, imprisonment, and traveling distance, among other reasons. As of yet, no misuse has been reported.[79]

There are a number of advantages that have been accredited to the use of videotaped depositions. Susan Carlson notes five of these advantages.[80] Since one may not accurately remember information over long periods of time, the deposition can be taken close to the event and preserved for later use. Secondly, videotape preserves the testimony of witnesses who die or move away. A third advantage is that perishable evidence may be preserved on tape. Fourth, viewing the taped testimony may refresh the memory of the attorneys. Finally, the taped testimony of witnesses who are unable to come to court provides the added information of the witness' demeanor that would otherwise have been lost.[81]

Thomas J. Murray, Jr., and Ohio attorney, offers several additional advantages of this use of videotape.[82] One advantage Murray notes is the alleviation of scheduling problems, particularly for medical experts or unavailable witnesses. In addition, he views the videotapes as allowing for better preparation by attorneys, consequently providing more effective presentations. Thirdly, the client can be better prepared for trial when he or she is aware of who the key witnesses are ahead of time. Prerecorded testimony, he points out, can be presented in its proper order providing for a more understandable presentation for the jury. Another advantage is that inadmissible and irrelevant material can be edited ahead of time, both improving the trial itself and reducing risk of mistrial. Also, the monitor can be placed in front of the jury so the testimony can be both seen and heard better. Finally, Murray cites the fact that jurors have relayed that videotaped testimony holds their attention bettern than a live presentation.

Unlike the overwhelming support given to the use of videotaped depositions, the use of videotaped trials is being debated. There are two ways videotaping is used at trials, and therefore two separate issues to evaluate. One method used is known as PRVTT, that is, prerecorded videotaped trials. With PRVTT all of the testimony is recorded at the convenience of the parties involved. Once the taping is completed a conference is held by the judge and attorneys to discuss motions and objections. The tape will then be edited according to the instructions of the judge. The edited tape is shown to the jury, while the master tape is stored for appeal purposes.[83] The second way videotaping is used is simply to record the trial while in progress as a substitute for a written transcript.

The first uses of videotapes at trials to exmaine is the PRVTT. A number of advantages are attributed to PRVTT for the judicial system, witnesses, and for the jurors. One advantage for the judicial system is that recording ahead of time provides for a concise presentation at trial. This allows for a clear presentation and knowledge of the length of trial. By knowing how long the trial will take, court managemnet can be improved. By pre-recording the testimony, delays for waiting for witnesses can be avoided. This pre-recording also allows for the judge to consider the issues without being under pressure. He is also freed up to attend to other matters while the jurors are watching on tape. This system provides for much greater flexibility in the schedules of attorneys, and allows them more time to prepare motions. By knowing exactly what the evidence is, attorneys can question potential jurors more efficiently in the voir dire. One last benefit to the judicial system is that attorneys are able to prepare closing statements, under more relaxed time constraints, that are more complementary to their opening statements.[84]

The witnesses are benefited under this system in two ways. One is that their testimony can be recorded at their own convenience. The second, is that the recording can be done in an atmosphere that is comfortable for them, minus the distractions of a courtroom setting.[85]

The third significant party to benefit under this system is the juror. Jurors can foreknow how much time will be spent with the trial. The length of time spent is also greatly reduced. For example, the case *McCall v. Clemens* was viewed by the jury in two hours and forty minutes. This same case, if viewed in the traditional method, would have taken five days. Consequently, jurors spend less time away from their jobs and other responsibilities under this system. This also discourages the fatigue that the juror might experience at a normal trial proceeding. The actual viewing of the tape offers several improvements as well. For one, it is ordered logically. Another is that all irrelevant material is deleted. A third is that a zoom lens may be used to facilitate seeing detailed charts, etc.

Even with all of the strengths that have been listed in support of PRVTT's there are critics who point out its several disadvantages. The most significant criticism concerns the altered role of the judge in such trials. Rather than actively participating in the trial he would review portions of the videotape. Irving Kosky criticizes this changed role in his statement;

> "The judge's presence during a trial is essential. Judges play a role that varies from slightly active to very active,

depending upon the abilities of the
attorneys before them and the responses
and actions of the witness. Judges frequently point out areas that need clari-
fication, and their firm, guiding hand is
needed to control and expedite the trial.
The trained wisdom of our judiciary is
the most valuable asset of our system of
jurisprudence. To exclude judges from
participating actively in trials would be
to tamper with the very soul of democracy.[86]

Samuel Brackel warns that the ramification of
this change are expansive. Some of the projected effects of the absence of the judge in the
courtroom are decreased dignity and increased
likelihood of witnesses falsifying statements.[87]
    Apart from the changed role of the judge
there are several other criticisms of PRVTT's.
Former United States Attorney General Ramsey
Clark expressed that the impersonal nature of
the videotape would encourage a less, "sensitive
human evaluation."[88] The videotape also lends
itself to distortions. This may enhance view-
ers' tendencies to favor attractive participants. Although the videotaped proceeding has
been praised for its speed, this is also a point
of criticism. The intensity of the shorter proceedings may make it difficult for the jurors to
absorb all significant information.[89] The last
major criticism pertains to the expense of time
and money involved in these proceedings. With
PRVTT's there are the added costs of the materials and technicians for taping and editing over
and above routine trial expenses. It has been

estimated that one day of taping on location could range from $440 to $1568. If a written transcript is desired there would be an additional cost of $2.25 per page rate for an original and copy. In some cases the editing time may be up to two and one half that of the original recording.[90] All of these factors have contributed to the slow reception of PRVTT's into the judicial system.

The last use of videotapes in the courts that will be discussed is for the purpose of providing a record of the trial. Here videotapes replace written transcripts. The real concern about the use of these videotapes is their usability at appellate proceedings. It was thought that the instant availability of the transcript would be beneficial for appeals. The results of using videotapes for appellate review have been unfavorable. One reason is the length of time consumed from reviewing the tape as opposed to reading a transcript. In one instance it took fifteen and one half hours to review a tape while the written transcript of the same trial took only five hours to review. In addition to the time factor involved, judges preferred reading the transcripts at their own convenience to viewing the tape en masse.[91] Judges also found it more difficult to compare one portion of the record with another when recorded on tape.[92] If a written transcript is to be taken from a videotape it is considerably more time-consuming, and consequently more expensive, than when taken from stenographic notes. A typist averages only 20-25 pages a day when transcribing from the videotape whereas he or she can type 80-120 pages of copy from stenographic notes. These inconveniences and costs involved with the videotaped transcripts have led to two states discontinuing the practice.

Depending upon their particular use, videotapes have either gained wide support or clear rejection in the courts. The trends consequently seem clear. As can be seen in the Erie County experience, videotaped depositions have much to offer the courts both to improve their efficiency and to enhance the preservation of testimony. There is no question about the advantages outweighing the disadvantages of this use of technology. PRVTT's are more controversial. However, as the system is refined its usage will continue to expand.[93] Even so, pre-recorded trials will never completely replace conventional trials.[94] The use of videotapes for transcript purposes so far has been unsuccessful. Until the burden of maintaining both a written and video copy of the trial record no longer outweights its benefits, this will not be widely used in the courts.

CONCLUSION

Reform efforts have been instituted in the American court systems ever since Roscoe Pound established the need for such efforts in his speech to the American Bar Association in 1906. With the problems of congestion, sentencing practices, and the protection of individual rights there continues to be efforts to improve the functioning of the courts. Three of the presently being tried are: unification of the courts, merit selection of judges, and videotaping various court proceedings. Although it is

not a panacea, court unification offers a means
to eliminate waste and enhance coordination in
state judicial systems. Consequently, unification efforts appear to be expanding. Merit selection of the judiciary offers a means to select more highly qualified judges apart from the
political practices that often accompany
elections. This too seems to be growing in pop-
ularity. Although great hopes for reform are
placed in each of these efforts little empirical
research has been conducted to clearly establish
the validity of the claims of their proponents.
The third reform effort addressed, videotaping,
offers promise for improved court proceedings in
keeping with the advances of modern technology.
Videotaped depositions have been lauded almost
universally.[95] Precorded videotaped trials
have received mixed acceptance. However, there
seems to be a future for their use in the court
system. Videotapes for appellate use have so
far been impractical. All three of these reform
efforts are continually being implemented as a
means of improving the effectiveness and efficiency of the courts. As these measures are refined and research is conducted it seems they
will aid the courts in performing their functions in society.

APPENDIX: A

MODELS OF STATE COURT ORGANIZATION [96]

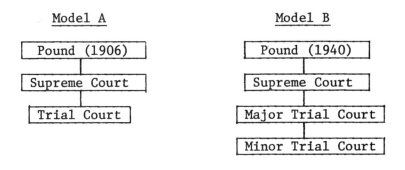

Model A

Pound (1906)
Supreme Court
Trial Court

Model B

Pound (1940)
Supreme Court
Major Trial Court
Minor Trial Court

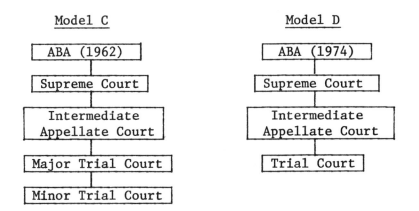

Model C

ABA (1962)
Supreme Court
Intermediate Appellate Court
Major Trial Court
Minor Trial Court

Model D

ABA (1974)
Supreme Court
Intermediate Appellate Court
Trial Court

[1] Sarat, Austin. The role of courts and the logic of court reform: notes on the Justice Department's approach to improving justice. *Judicature*. 1981, 64, 300-311.

[2] *Houston Chronicle*, November 19, 1982, p. 11.

[3] Pound, Roscoe. The causes of popular disatisfaction with the administration of justice. *Journal of the American Judicature Society*, 1937, 20, p. 178-187.

[4] Pursley, Robert D. *Introduction to Criminal Justice*. (2nd ed.). New York: MacMillan Publishing Co., Inc., 1980, p. 326.

[5] Berkson, Larry C., Hays, Steven, Carlson, Susan J. *Managing the State Courts*. St. Paul, MN: West Publishing Company, 1977, p.8.

[6] Ibid., p. 8-9.

[7] Ibid., p. 9.

[8] Vanderbilt, Arthur T. *Improving the Administration of Justice -- Two Decades of Development*. Cincinnati, College of Law University of Cincinnati, 1957, p. 5-6, 78.

[9] Berkson, Hays, Carlson, p. 11.

[10] President's Commission on Law Enforcement and Administration of Justice. *Task force report: the courts*. Washington, Government Printing Office, 1967.

[11] Berkson, Hays, Carlson, p. 12.

[12] Broder, Josef M., Porter, John F., & Smathers, Webb M. The hidden consequences of court unification. *Judicature*, 1981, 65, p. 10.

[13] Pound, Roscoe, Principles and outline of a modern unified court organization. *Journal of the American Judicature Society*. 1940, 23 p. 223.

[14] Hays, Seven W. The logic of court reform: is Frederick Tayor gloating? *Criminal Justice Review*. 1979, 4, p. 8.

[15] Berkson, Hays, Carlson, p. 104.

[16] Tarr, G. Allen. Court unification and court performance: a preliminary assessment. *Judicature*, 1981, 64, p. 358.

[17] Ibid.

[18] Ibid., p. 362.

[19] Vanderbilt, p. 17.

[20] Berkson, Larry C. The emerging ideal of court unification. *Judicature*, 1977, 60, p. 374-5.

[21] Ashman, Allan; Parness, Jeffrey. The concept of a unified court system. *DePaul Law Review*, 1974, 24, p. 29-30.

[22] Berkson, 1977, p. 375.

[23] Broder, Porter, & Smathers, p. 15.

[24] Tarr, p. 362.

[25] Berkson, 1977, p. 376-377.

[26] Tarr, p. 363.

[27] Ibid., p. 362.

[28] Pound, 1940, p. 229.

[29] Berkson, 1977, p. 378.

[30] Ibid., p. 379.

[31] Ibid.

[32] Ibid.

[33] Tarr, p. 362.

[34] Berkson, 1977, p. 379-381.

[35] Ibid., p. 381.

[36] Tarr, p. 363.

[37] Berkson, 1977, p. 382.

[38] Tarr, p. 363.

[39] Hays, 1979, p. 10.

[40] Ibid.

[41] Gallas, Geoff. The conventional wisdom of state court administration. *Jusice System*

Journal, 1976, 2, p. 30.

[42] Broder, Porter & Smathers, p. 12.

[43] Hayes, 1979, p. 10.

[44] Ibid.

[45] Ibid.

[46] Ibid., p. 11.

[47] Gallas, Geoff. Court reform: has it been built on an adequate foundation. *Judicature*, 1979, 63, p. 30.

[48] Broder, Porter & Smathers, p. 11.

[49] Ibid., p. 113.

However, those who acknowledge and support such a trend, viewing unification as a viable alternative to existing court systems, emphasize that unification *alone* will not be a panacea for all of the existing problems in the courts.[50]

[50] Gazell, James A. *The Future of State Court Management*. Port Washington, NY: National University Publications, 1978, p. 25-26.

[51] Pursley, p. 300.

[52] Friesen, Ernest C., Jr; Gallas, Edward C.; & Gallas, Nesta M. *Managing the Courts*. Indianapolis: The Bobbs-Merrill Company, Inc., 1971, p. 53.

[53] Berkson, Larry C. Judicial selection in the United States: a special report. *Judicature*, 1980, 64, p. 176.

[54] Vanderbilt, p. 14.

[55] Berkson, 1980, p. 176-177.

[56] Pound, 1937.

[57] Berkson, 1980, p. 177.

[58] Carlson, 1980, p. 215.

[59] Pursley, p. 333.

[60] Berkson, 1980, p. 178.

[61] Ibid., p. 176.

[62] Berkson, Hays, Carlson, p. 136.

[63] Berkson, 1977, p. 136-137.

[64] Pursley, p. 334.

[65] Vanderbilt, p. 16.

[66] Jenkins, William, Jr. Retention elections: who wins when no one loses. *Judicature*, 1977, 61, p. 80.

[67] The dictatorship of irrelevancy. *Journal of the American Judicature Society*, 1964, 48, p. 124.

[68] Pursley, p. 334.

[69] Berkson, Hays, Carlson, p. 139.

[70] Crockett, George W., Jr. Judicial selection and the black experience. *Judicature*, 1975, 58, p. 438-482.

[71] McKnight, R. Neal; Schafer, Roger; Johnson, Charles A. Choosing judges: do the voters know what they're doing. *Judicature*. 1978, 62, p. 98.

[72] Berkson, Hays, Carlson, p. 140.

[73] Ibid.

[74] Ibid., p. 138.

[75] James, Howard. *Crisis in the Courts*. New York: David McKay Company, Inc., 1971, p. viii.

[76] Salvan, Sherwood A. Videotape for the community. *Judicature, 1975, 59, p. 222.*

[77] Salvan, p. 222.

[78] Murray, Thomas J., Jr. Videotaped depositions: the Ohio experience. *Judicature*, 1978, 61, p. 259.

[79] Ibid.

[80] Berkson, Hays, Carlson, p. 297.

[81] Ibid., p 297-298.

[82] Murray, p. 261.

[83] Berkson, Hays, Carlson, p. 299.

[84] Ibid., p. 300-301.

[85] Ibid., p. 301.

[86] Kosky, Irving. Videotape in Ohio. *Judicature*, 1975, 59, p. 236.

[87] Berkson, Hays, Carlson, p. 302.

[88] Kosky, p. 237.

[89] Berkson, Hays, Carlson, p. 303.

[90] Kosky, p. 236.

[91] Berkson, Hays, Carlson, p. 403.

[92] Kosky, p. 233.

[93] Salvan, p. 228.

[94] McCrystal, James L. Videotaped trials: a primer. *Judicature*, 1978, 61, p. 255.

[95] Berkson, Hays, Carlson, p. 297.

[96] Berkson, 1977, p. 376.

INDEX

ABOUT THE EDITORS

Sloan T. Letman currently serves as Dean of the Social Sciences and Associate Professor of Criminal Justice at Loyola University of Chicago. He received his B.A. in Sociology and M.A. in Urban Studies from Loyola, and the Juris Doctor degree from the DePaul University College of Law.

Dan W. Edwards is Director of Graduate Studies in the School of Social Work at Southern University in New Orleans, Louisiana. He received his B.S., M.S.W., and Ph.D. degrees from Florida State University. Dr. Edwards was formerly Chairman of the fields of Social Work Practice and Corrections at Louisiana State University.

Daniel J. Bell is presently Chairman of the Department of Criminal Justice at Southeast Texas State University. He received his B.S., M.S., and Ph.D. degrees from the University of Oregon. Dr. Bell was formerly Director of Graduate Studies in the Department of Criminal Justice at Kent State University.

CONTRIBUTORS

Alfreda Talton-Harris, J.D.
  Assistant Professor, Youngstown State University

G. Larry Mays, Ph.D.
  Chairman, Department of Criminal Justice, New Mexico State University

Carolyn Watkins Marsh, J.D.
  Associate Professor, Department of Legal Studies, Sangamon State University

B. Grant Stitt, Ph.D.
  Assistant Professor, Department of Criminal Justice, Memphis State University

Donna Hutchison, Ph.D.
  Assistant Professor, Department of Criminal Justice, Memphis State University

Daniel J. Bell, Ph.D.
  Chairman, Department of Criminal Justice, Southwest Texas State University

Sloan T. Letman, J.D.
  Associate Professor, Department of Criminal Justice, Loyola University of Chicago

Betty Crews, Ph.D.
    Instructor, Department of Criminal Justice,
    Sam Houston State University